THE

GOLF

LOVER'S GUIDE TO

ENGLAND

Dedicated to all golf club employees for their commitment and endeavour, ensuring our courses are always ready for play whatever nature throws at us, providing the warmest welcome to each and every visitor. Thank you.

THE
GOLF
LOVER'S GUIDE TO
ENGLAND

Michael Whitehead

WHITE OWL
AN IMPRINT OF PEN & SWORD BOOKS LTD.
YORKSHIRE – PHILADELPHIA

First published in Great Britain in 2020 by
PEN & SWORD WHITE OWL
An imprint of
Pen & Sword Books Ltd
Yorkshire - Philadelphia

ISBN 9781526756329

The right of Michael Whitehead to be identified as
Author of this work has been asserted by him in
accordance with the Copyright, Designs and Patents Act
1988. A CIP catalogue record for this book is available
from the British Library.

Typeset by SJmagic DESIGN SERVICES, India.
Printed and bound in India by Replika Press Pvt. Ltd.

Pen & Sword Books Limited incorporates the imprints
of Atlas, Archaeology, Aviation, Discovery, Family
History, Fiction, History, Maritime, Military, Military
Classics, Politics, Select, Transport, True Crime, Air
World, Frontline Publishing, Leo Cooper, Remember
When, Seaforth Publishing, The Praetorian Press,
Wharncliffe Local History, Wharncliffe Transport,
Wharncliffe True Crime and White Owl.

For a complete list of Pen & Sword titles please contact
PEN & SWORD BOOKS LIMITED
47 Church Street, Barnsley, South Yorkshire, S70 2AS,
United Kingdom
E-mail: enquiries@pen-and-sword.co.uk
Website: www.pen-and-sword.co.uk

Or
PEN AND SWORD BOOKS
1950 Lawrence Rd, Havertown, PA 19083, USA
E-mail: Uspen-and-sword@casematepublishers.com
Website: www.penandswordbooks.com

Cover images:
Front cover: St Enodoc – Church Course, 16th hole.
jameslovettphotography.com

Royal Birkdale 18th green & clubhouse. *Royal Birkdale Golf Club*

Back cover: 4th green, West Sussex Golf Club.
kevinmurraygolfphotography.com

MIX
Paper from
responsible sources
FSC® C016779

CONTENTS

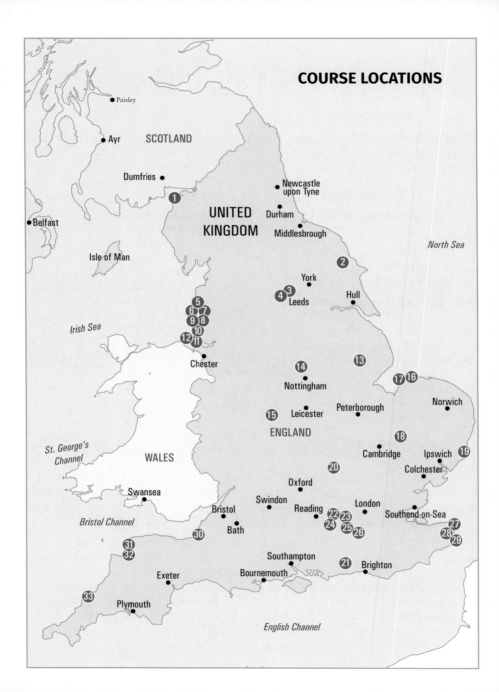

COURSE LOCATIONS

KEYS

1. Silloth On Solway Golf Club
2. Ganton Golf Club
3. Alwoodley Golf Club
4. Moortown Golf Club
5. Royal Lytham & St Annes Golf Club
6. Royal Birkdale Golf Club
7. Hillside Golf Club
8. Southport & Ainsdale Golf Club
9. Formby Golf Club
10. The West Lancashire Golf Club
11. Wallasey Golf Club
12. Royal Liverpool Golf Club
13. Woodhall Spa, The National Golf Centre – Hotchkin Course
14. Hollinwell
15. The Belfry Hotel & Resort – Brabazon Course
16. Royal West Norfolk Golf Club
17. Hunstanton Golf Club
18. Royal Worlington & Newmarket Golf Club
19. Aldeburgh Golf Club – The Championship Course
20. Woburn Golf Club
21. West Sussex Golf Club
22. Swinley Forest Golf Club
23. Sunningdale Golf Club
24. The Berkshire Golf Club
25. St George's Hill Golf Club
26. Walton Heath Golf Club
27. Prince's Golf Club
28. The Royal St George's Golf Club
29. Royal Cinque Ports Golf Club
30. Burnham & Berrow Golf Club – The Championship Course
31. Saunton Golf Club – East Course
32. The Royal North Devon Golf Club, Westward Ho!
33. St Enodoc Golf Club – Church Course

INTRODUCTION

ABOUT THIS GUIDE

With over 2,000 courses to choose from, planning a golf trip in England can be an exciting but equally challenging task. Where should you go? How do you book? When can you play?

This comprehensive guide is devoted to some of England's finest golf courses available for visitors to play. Within each dedicated chapter you will find everything you need including general course information, contact details, how to book a round and *when* you can book a round as a visitor. There is also a homage to the rich and varied history of each course and its club along with a useful outline of how best to approach playing the course.

A number of clubs within this guide have more than one golf course, which deserve equal mention and merit. Overall, there are thirty-three in-depth chapters featuring thirty-five 18-hole courses, two 27-hole courses and one for a 'sacred' 9-hole course.

The chapters are divided into regional sections, starting from the North of England, traversing down to the South. In each section, you'll find additional information on other golf clubs nearby (typically no more than 20–25 minutes' drive unless stated otherwise) along with a further selection of both 18- and 9-hole courses located within the region.

For those who like to take every opportunity to play as often as you can, over as many different types of courses while on your golfing travels, there's plenty to digest.

Here are some general points to consider when reading through the guide:

Green fees. Course green fees are generally subject to change on an annual basis. In order to preserve the validity of the

Acknowledgements

I'd like to thank the following people, who gave up their valuable time to ensure each course chapter was accurate and up to date. Their cooperation and hospitality were greatly appreciated:

Elaine Twissell and Mark Duncalf (Royal Lytham & St Annes Golf Club), Michael Sawicki (Royal Birkdale Golf Club), Doreen Francey, John Heggarty, Sam Cooper and Simon Newland (Royal Liverpool Golf Club), John Mort and Mike Adams (Wallasey Golf Club), Gareth Glynne-Jones and Stuart Leech (Formby Golf Club), Jim Payne and Frances Edwards (Southport & Ainsdale Golf Club), Chris Alty (The West Lancashire Golf Club), Chris Williams, Tash Neal and Matt Duncalf (Hillside Golf Club), Tim Checketts and Robert Leigh (The Royal St George's Golf Club), James Leah and Andrew Reynolds (Royal Cinque Ports Golf Club), John Kilshaw (West Sussex Golf Club), Glenna Beasley (Woburn Golf Club), George Ritchie (Swinley Forest Golf Club), Stuart Christie, Jemma Overing, Simon Peaford and Gordon Simpson (Walton Heath Golf Club), Christian Foreman and Richard Andrews (Sunningdale Golf Club), Adrian Smith and Paul Anderson (The Berkshire Golf Club), Julie Slater and John Green (Alwoodley Golf Club), Peter Rishworth (Moortown Golf Club), Gary Pearce and Gary Brown (Ganton Golf Club), Alan Oliver (Silloth On Solway Golf Club), Mark Evans (Royal North Devon Golf Club), Simon Greatorex (St Enodoc Golf Club), Jon Sutherland (Saunton Golf Club), Karen Drake, David Haines, Jack Palmer and Stuart Norton-Collins (Burnham and Berrow Golf Club), Richard Latham (Woodhall Spa, The National Golf Centre), David Wybar (Aldeburgh Golf Club), Tim Stephens, Jessie Brown and Simon Rayner (Royal West Norfolk Golf Club), Martyn Bonner MBE and Oliver Baines (Hollinwell), Caroline Froggatt (The Belfry Hotel & Resort), Chris White (Hunstanton Golf Club), Scott Ballentine (Royal Worlington & Newmarket Golf Club), Ali McGuirk (Prince's Golf Club), Christine Riggs and James Collier (St George's Hill Golf Club).

I'd like to express my particular gratitude to the following:

Philip Truett, historian at Walton Heath for spending an hour with me on the telephone talking in such affectionate terms about his wonderful golf club and its rich history.

John Kilshaw, much admired member of West Sussex Golf Club, for his kindness and hospitality both during and after our round of golf.

Matthew Rose (Aldeburgh) and Graeme Roberts (Swinley Forest) for selflessly answering a total stranger's cry for help on social media and capturing a series of wonderful photographs of their beloved course.

Steve Carr (www.stevecarrgolf.com), Kevin Diss (www.kevindiss.com), David Cannon (Getty Images), James Lovett (jameslovettphotography.com), Jason Livy (www.jasonlivy.com), James Drake (specialist golf course photographer, Northern England) and Kevin Murray (www.kevinmurraygolfphotography.com) for kindly permitting the use of a number of images from their fabulous collections within the guide.

Neil Laird, whose website – www.scottishgolfhistory.org – once again provided terrific insight regarding the history of golf in England and its origins.

My old friend Neville Benbow who spent three days toiling through a rough first draft of my manuscript, pointing out more grammatical errors than a professional writer would care to mention.

My publisher Pen & Sword, in particular Jonathan Wright, Janet Brookes, Emily Robinson, Charlie Simpson, Aileen Pringle and Karyn Burnham.

To my wife, Kellie and our children, Hermione, Charlie and James. And to my parents, Anita & Peter. I thank my lucky stars each day to have such a loving, supportive family who put up with my golfing shenanigans. Last one, I promise ... (until the next one).

information within this guide, colour-coded price bandings have been applied to each course chapter. These bandings are for indication purposes only and based on 2020-2021 prices.

It is recommended to check directly with the course in order to confirm the exact green fee for the time of year you are planning to book.

Price Guide:
- up to £49
- £50 – £99
- £100 – £149
- £150 – £200
- over £200

(Actual green fees – based on the latest available prices – have been included for 9-hole courses)

High Season. *May-September
Shoulder Season. *April and October
Low Season. *November-March
(* = High/shoulder/low golf seasons in England are typically split within these months. Please check directly with each course to confirm.)

Booking Options. Most courses provide visitors with three ways to book a round of golf – online, phone or e-mail. Clubs generally prefer either phone or online booking. In the case of booking via e-mail, be sure to include all relevant details – preferred dates/times and the size of your group.

Distance/yardage. The measurements given in this guide for the length of each course, and longest and shortest holes, are from the shortest to the longest tee-boxes. All distances are in yards (yds). In some cases, the longest tees are reserved for championships or members only. Most golf clubs have a selection of tees available and the starter at the course will offer advice, based on your handicap, as to which tee you should use. For a more enjoyable round, it is wise to heed this advice.

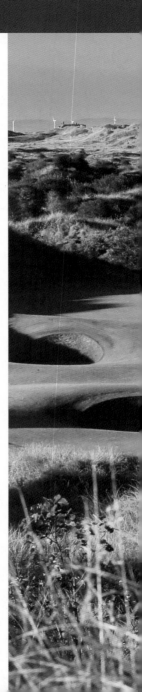

Handicap certificate. While many courses have a laid back approach to checking handicap certificates, and may not even ask for them, it is better to be safe than sorry by making sure it's available. The aim is not to check the handicap of every golfer, but rather to maintain the pace of play on the course and an expectation to keep up with that.

Caddies. If you book a caddie, be aware that they usually work on a self-employed basis and expect to be paid directly in cash. Currently, you should expect to pay between £50–£60 plus gratuity to use their services. The amount of gratuity is discretionary but around 20 per cent would usually be the minimum starting point.

Equipment hire. Most courses have a range of equipment available for visitors to use – trolleys, clubs etc. If you require a buggy on health/medical grounds it is advised to book in advance, as there will be a limited number available. The fees for equipment hire may be subject to change on an annual basis and will vary from club to club, however, on average you should expect to pay:

£5 – £7   for pull trolleys
£10 – £20   for electric trolleys
£30 – £35   for clubs
£30 – £35   for buggies

As with green fees, it is best to check with the course when booking to confirm the price and availability of items to hire.

Dress Code. Standard golfing attire is required in order to play the courses listed within this guide. It is recommended to check with each course to confirm if any specific rules apply (long socks when wearing shorts, for example).

If you're planning on dining at the clubhouse before or after your round, it is also best to check with the respective course whether there are any rules on formal lounge wear before you travel. Jeans and non-golfing sports attire are pretty much a no-no wherever you go.

Visitor tee-times*. All the golf clubs featured in this guide welcome visitors at specific times during the week. Visitor tee-times are outlined in the first section of each chapter.

Ensure you arrive at least thirty minutes before your tee-time in order to finalise any outstanding points regarding your booking (payments etc.). Most courses have practice facilities for you to warm up before you head to the first tee.

(* = As a result of global events during 2020 and subsequent government guidance, visitor tee-times may temporarily differ from those stated within each chapter, therefore, it is worth confirming with each club when planning your visit.)

A BRIEF HISTORY OF GOLF IN ENGLAND

Despite several offers for her hand and numerous failed courtships, Elizabeth I remained unmarried throughout her life. With no immediate heir, the House of Tudor's dynastic reign came to an end following her death in 1603. Subsequently, James VI of Scotland ascended to the throne, becoming James I of England and Ireland.

The first dual monarch of England and Scotland made his way down to London accompanied by a large entourage, which included a number of noblemen, many of whom regularly engaged in a particular sporting activity well known in Scotland but relatively unheard of south of the border – golf.

Due to a lack of documentary evidence from the time, the exact location of where golf was first played in England is somewhat disputed, but there's little doubt that it involved the king (himself a keen enthusiast of the game) and his courtiers.

While en route to claim his new crown, King James I made an overnight stop in the town of Royston (approximately forty-five miles north of London) and became so enthralled with the surrounding rural area and its suitability for hunting, he decreed significant amounts of money to be spent on appropriate lodgings in order to accommodate him on a regular basis.

Royston was certainly where the very first game of golf in England was officially recorded (almost nineteen years after King James' stopover) on 4 October 1624, between George

Villiers, 1st Earl of Buckingham and Sir Robert Deale. Villiers documented the match in his accounts:

> Paid to the Gofball keep(er) for clubs and balles at
>   Roiston 4th October (1624) £1 11s 0d.
> Lost to Sir Robert Deale at Goff the 4th October (1624)
>   £2 0s 0d.
>
> Source: www.scottishgolfhistory.org

Villiers also notes further expenditure in other accounts after this date for the purchase of numerous pieces of golf equipment (golf clubs are actually referred to as bats or 'battes').

As Villiers was a firm favourite of King James I (it was he who granted an Earldom to Villiers) it is most likely that the earl was introduced to golf through their relationship. Nearby Therfield Heath (within walking distance of the king's royal lodge and, since 1892, the home of Royston Golf Club) is cited as an ideal location – with its topography very reminiscent to that of a links course – for His Majesty to have played golf during his many visits to Royston.

There is, however, no suggestion (or evidence) that King James I was involved in the game between Villiers and Deale as, by 1624, his health was already in steep decline.

In all likelihood, the king and members of his court would have looked for appropriate areas where they could continue playing their beloved game soon after arriving in London. The boroughs of Richmond and Blackheath have both held longstanding claims of their own to be the original sites where golf was first played in England.

A French Ambassador noted in 1606 observing Prince Henry (the king's youngest son) playing a game similar to 'jeu de maille' – a lawn game involving a mallet and a ball – in the grounds of Richmond Palace. As 'jeu de maille' (mallet game) was not a sport widely practised outside of France, the young prince was more likely to have been playing golf.

The Royal Blackheath Golf Club has consistently maintained that it was first 'instituted' in 1608. This claim relies heavily on a number of anecdotes also relating to Prince

Henry – one of which involves him nearly hitting his tutor with a golf ball – dated on or around this time and alleged to have taken place near to Greenwich Palace, where King James spent much of his time during his reign. However, no official records exist to substantiate these assertions (or precisely when or where they may have happened).

The earliest surviving record of any active golfing society in England dates back to 1766 when the Honourable Company of Golfers at Blackheath (as it was then known) were presented with a silver club to be used for a competition. This still makes Royal Blackheath the oldest golf club both in England and anywhere outside Scotland.

Westward Ho!, originally a fictional seaside setting for Charles Kingsley's celebrated novel of the same name, published in 1855, subsequently became a real-life tourist hotspot and home to the oldest surviving golf course in England. In 1860, the great doyen of course design, Old Tom Morris, was persuaded to spend a month away from Prestwick in order to sprinkle some of his stardust over the rugged links land.

The course at Westward Ho! has been home to The Royal North Devon Golf Club since its formation in 1864 and was where John Henry (J.H) Taylor – member of golf's great triumvirate alongside James Braid and Harry Vardon – learnt how to play the game. Taylor, born in nearby Northam, would go on to become a five-time Champion Golfer of the Year.

After Westward Ho!, golf's expansion throughout England continued unabated. Prompted by the development of the railway, new clubs and courses were built and formed mainly within walking distance of stations located all across the country; along the north west coast, Yorkshire, London's surrounding sandbelt, and the south east.

During this golden era a group of budding designers would emerge, leaving behind their chosen professions in order to pursue a new creative vision. In the process, they would shape the future of golf course architecture for the next century.

Chief amongst them was a newly qualified lawyer, and former captain of the Cambridge University Golf Club by the name of Henry Shapland "Harry" Colt. Under the tutelage of

his golfing mentor, Douglas Rolland (James Braid's uncle), Colt would design a new golf course across links land at Camber, near Rye, in 1894.

After six years as Rye's honorary secretary, Colt moved closer to London becoming the first secretary of the newly formed Sunningdale Golf Club. Whilst there, he became inspired by the work of Willie Park Jr. on land traditionally seen as unsuitable for a golf course and would later add a series of popular re-designs to the original layout.

From his base in the heart of the Surrey/Berkshire sandbelt, Colt would spread his architectural wings building new heathland courses nearby at Swinley Forest and St George's Hill. Returning to Sunningdale in 1922 he would create his own 18-hole design alongside the existing layout. For many, the Old and New courses at Sunningdale represent the finest combined 36-hole heathland experience you can find. However, Harry Colt was by no means a sole pioneer in his field.

A few miles down the road from Sunningdale, the founding members of Walton Heath Golf Club, led by Sir Henry Cosmo Bonsor, were on the lookout for an architect to build their new course. Going against all conventional advice, Bonsor would appoint his brother-in-law – Herbert Fowler, a man from a banking background and with no previous golf course design experience.

Whether or not his appointment was prompted by Bonsor in order to assist a family member during a period of financial difficulty, Fowler would repay any debt he owed in spades, delivering two of the very finest heathland courses (the Old course opened in 1904, swiftly followed by the New in 1907). At the grand old age of seventy-one Herbert would bookend his glittering career with another 36-hole heathland masterpiece, this time at The Berkshire (the Blue and Red courses both opened for play at the same time in 1928).

Meanwhile, further north in Leeds, a local medical practitioner would also take his first steps into the world of golf course design. In 1907, as a founding member of Alwoodley Golf Club, Dr Alister MacKenzie volunteered to construct the new course. After being given the seal of approval from Harry Colt, MacKenzie did not have to look far for his second project, just across the road at Moortown.

Many more golf clubs in England and throughout the world would seek the services of the 'course doctor' (Cypress Point, Pasatiempo and Royal Melbourne to name just a few). He is, without doubt, remembered most fondly for accepting an invitation from the great Bobby Jones to lay down a new course in his native U.S state of Georgia.

Sadly, Dr MacKenzie never got to see Augusta National in all its glory nor the famous tournament for which it is synonymous. His last visit to the course was in 1932, six months prior to completion. He died in January 1934, two months before the inaugural Augusta National Invitation Tournament, now known as The Masters.

Royal St George's would have the honour of hosting the first Open Championship outside of Scotland in 1894 (won by J.H Taylor), swiftly followed three years later by Royal Liverpool. In all, England has hosted The Open on fifty occasions (up to 2020) across six different venues.

England has also played a major role in the development of international-team tournaments. Royal Cromer holds the distinction of hosting the first ever international golf match in 1905. This informal meeting between teams from the U.S.A and Great Britain – designed to

promote international friendships in the world of women's golf - was the pre-cursor to the Curtis Cup.

The origins of another famous team event can be traced along England's golf coast. In 1921 a friendly match between American and British golfers acted as a curtain raiser to the Amateur Championship, held that year at Royal Liverpool, sowing the seeds for what would become the Walker Cup. In 2019 the tournament returned to where it all began for the 47th edition, held at Hoylake for the second time in its history.

Moortown Golf Club officials were given just four months notice to prepare for the very first edition of the Ryder Cup to be held this side of the Atlantic in 1929 (nowadays venues are announced at least five years in advance). Until 2002 the biennial competition was held almost exclusively at English courses, when in Europe, with a total of ten different clubs hosting the event on fifteen separate occasions.

Fast-forward to the present day and England can now boast more than double the number of golf courses in both Scotland and Ireland combined, with a diverse range of layouts unmatched by any other territory outside the United States – links, heathland, parkland, moorland, woodland, inland links – they're all here in abundance.

Sharing a border with its spiritual home, England is undoubtedly golf's exquisite front garden.

THE NORTH

SILLOTH ON SOLWAY GOLF CLUB

The Club House,
Station Road, Silloth,
Wigton, Cumbria,
CA7 4BL
www.sillothgolfclub.co.uk
Phone: + 44 (0) 1697 331304
Email: office@sillothgolfclub.co.uk

General course information –
Par: 72 (Blue/White/Yellow) / 75 (Red)
S.S.S: 73 (Blue) / 72 (White) / 70 (Yellow) / 75 (Red)
Slope rating: 136 (Blue) / 133 (White) / 132 (Yellow) / 131 (Red)
Length: 5,806yds–6,641yds
Longest hole: Par-5 5th, 499yds–559yds / Par-5 17th, 464yds (Red)
Shortest hole: Par-3 9th, 110yds–142yds
Type: Links

Handicap Certificate: Not required

Green fees:
(Low season)
● per round (weekdays & weekends)
(Shoulder season)
● per round (weekdays)
● per round (weekends)
(High season)
● per round (weekdays & weekends)

Caddies: Not available

Equipment hire:
Clubs, buggies and trolleys all available via the pro shop +44 (0) 1697 332404.

How do I book a round of golf?
Silloth on Solway welcomes visitors at all times during the week to play the links course. Tee-times are available after 9.30 am midweek, 10.30 am Saturdays and after 11.30 am on Sundays.

There are three ways to book a round of golf at Silloth on Solway Golf Club:

Online:
www.sillothgolfclub.co.uk/Visitors/Book a tee time

Phone:
+44 (0) 1697 331304

Email:
bookings@sillothgolfclub.co.uk

Price Guide: ● up to £49 | ● £50 – £99 | ● £100 – £149 | ● £150 – £200 | ● over £200

HISTORY

In 1910, at just 19 years of age, Cecilia Leitch (more commonly known as Cecil) accepted an invitation to play a 72-hole match against two-time Men's Open champion, Harold Hilton, to be held at Walton Heath and Sunningdale. Hilton, seen as the golfing superstar of his day, was expected to win handily. However, young Cecil would shock her illustrious opponent – and a partisan crowd – winning 2&1.

Cecil would go on to claim victory in no less than twelve national tournaments, including four British Ladies Amateur Championships, and is now rightly regarded as one of the pioneers of women's golf.

Her playing style was in sharp contrast to other female golfers at the time, hitting the ball hard, straight and long. It was a style that served her well and one learnt the hard way from a tender age among the blustery surroundings of her local links course at Silloth on Solway Golf Club.

Formed in 1892 by the North British Railway Company as part of a wider expansion of Silloth to help promote the town as a popular tourist location, the original course was laid out by Davie Grant who learnt his

Steep slopes either side of a narrow green at the 4th hole (The Mill). Any approach shot must be handled with care. *Silloth On Solway Golf Club*

trade across the border at North Berwick. Grant's design, at just over 4,500yds, was described as 'sporting', which was a Victorian term for rough and hazardous.

In 1898 another East Lothian golfing resident, Willie Park Jr., would apply his expertise to bring the course into the modern era. Park's changes added over a thousand yards to the overall length and introduced a number of blind and semi-blind tee shots still in evidence today.

In 1915 Dr Alister MacKenzie was asked to cast his architectural eye over the course. However, the doctor's full design proposals would not find universal agreement among the club committee, with only his changes to the third green and fourth tee gaining their approval. Both of these MacKenzie alterations remain to this day.

PLAYING THE COURSE

When you reach the 5th tee of this fascinating links course just forget about golf for a few seconds and take a good look around you. Here is where you find answers aplenty to the one nagging question that comes up time and time again about Silloth, isolated as it is away from England's golfing hotspots; is it worth the trip?

On a clear day, you'll see the Isle of Man on the horizon about sixty miles out in the middle of the Irish Sea. On your left sit two of the highest mountains in England – Scafell Pike (*the* highest) and Skiddaw - carved along the northwest tip of England's Lake District. Across the Solway Firth lies the awe-inspiring landscape of Dumfries and Galloway.

There are many, many reasons why this particular golf journey will always be worth it and the panorama that greets you here is most definitely one of them. At Silloth on Solway, Mother Nature definitely keeps her side of the bargain.

Thanks to the efforts of Messrs Grant, Park Jr. and Dr MacKenzie, the course doesn't let you down either. Full of character and intrigue from start to finish, it grabs hold of you on the first hole and refuses to let go until you make your last putt.

The course is a fairly traditional out and back layout usually playing into the wind on the front-9 and behind on the back-9. Only the 4th and 13th holes face the opposite direction both going out and coming back.

All the fun at the 1st hole begins with your approach, which is blind towards a sunken saucer-shaped green set into the sand dunes. Aim left with your drive for the best line over the plateau for your second shot. The opening hole is the perfect pre-cursor of how to score well on many of the longer holes at Silloth where the best policy is to land short and run up to the putting surface.

There are a few exceptions to this, particularly at the dogleg left, par-4, 3rd where the green is elevated so anything too short will simply roll back down the hill. The best line from the tee is along the left leaving you with a pitch up the slope. A putt from the back needs a steady hand towards the pin.

Your tee-shot on the par-4 4th is blind over a high ridge of sand dunes toward a bottleneck fairway. Trouble awaits behind the green with steep slopes left and right so either a high pitch or a bump and run approach needs to be right up the middle.

The 9th is only a short par-3 but often played into a stiff breeze with a green surrounded by pot bunkers. *Silloth On Solway Golf Club*

When you've finished admiring the stunning panorama at the 5th tee (take your time) you need to reach for the driver and aim your tee-shot right down the centre of the fairway. All the trouble here runs along the right so keep your approach toward the green along the left.

The 9th is a terrific short par-3 and is the signature hole on the front-9 offering another glimpse of the surroundings that will take your breath away. If the wind's blowing, choose your club wisely, nothing other than right at the centre will do. A par here is one you'll remember long after your round has finished.

The back-9 begins with a fabulous risk/reward dogleg left par-4 at the 10th. Big hitters can take on the corner to try and reach the green. Otherwise aim just beyond the two bunkers on the left of the fairway to leave a short pitch.

The 10th hole is called 'Blooming Heath'. The green is well guarded by bunkers left and right.
Silloth On Solway Golf Club

(13) SIGNATURE HOLE: PAR-5 13TH, 439YDS–511YDS, 'HOGS BACK'.

A short par-5 with no bunkers, this hole is an absolute enigma to all who play it, which is why so many see it as their favourite on a course with many worthy contenders.

Your tee-shot needs to be right down the middle towards the large elevated ridge. From this point, the shape of the fairway (hence the hole's name) can wreak havoc with your approach, deflecting what can look like the perfect shot off into deep heather and gorse on either side.

The 16th is the last par-3 which, due to its length and clever design, offers a tough choice between going straight for the elevated green or landing short and running up to the putting surface with your second shot. Bunkers left and right front wait for anything not on line.

The tee box at the par-5 17th sits in front of a wide valley the members like to call 'Duffers', ready to catch hold of any tired tee-shots – this is one place at Silloth where you're unlikely to appreciate the view so, if any motivation were needed, make sure your drive is straight and true.

The 18th is named after the late Viscount (William) Whitelaw, a long-standing member at Silloth and former president of the club until his death in 1999. The fairway is flanked with bunkers on the right and thick heather and gorse on the left. The long, narrow green has two bunkers at the front, so best to aim toward the back with your final approach.

18-hole courses nearby

● SEASCALE GOLF CLUB

A fine course with plenty of character, approximately one hour's drive south, down the coast road from Silloth. Formed in 1893, the links course at Seascale was originally created as a joint effort between Willie Campbell and George Lowe.

Website: www.seascalegolfclub.co.uk
Email: seascalegolfclub@gmail.com
Telephone: +44 (0) 1946 728202

Par: 71 / 74 (Red)
Length: 5,621yds–6,450yds
Type: Links

Fees:
● per round / day rate

● CARLISLE GOLF CLUB

Surrounded by mature parkland, this beautiful inland layout is regarded as one of the finest of its kind in the north of England. Founded in 1908, the course is regarded as a tough test for both low and high handicappers.

Website: carlislegolfclub.org
Email: secretary@carlislegolfclub.org
Telephone: +44 (0) 1228 513029

Par: 71 / 73 (Red)
Length: 5,562yds–6,249yds
Type: Parkland

Fees:
● per round (weekday)
● per round (weekend) / day rate

Lake District

● ULVERSTON GOLF CLUB

Lovely parkland course offering terrific views over Morecambe Bay and the Lake District. Originally created by Alex Herd (Champion Golfer of the Year, 1902) and redesigned by Harry Colt in the 1920s. (Limited availability for visitors on Tuesdays and Saturdays).

Website: www.ulverstongolf.co.uk
Email: enquiries@ulverstongolf.co.uk
Telephone: +44 (0) 1229 582824

Par: 71 / 74 (Red)
Length: 5,648yds–6,264yds
Type: Parkland

Fees:
● per round (weekday)
● per round (weekend)

● WINDERMERE GOLF CLUB

Set on high ground in the heart of the Lake District. The par-3 8th at Windermere provides unobstructed views across the incredible, surrounding landscape and is the signature hole on the course.

Website: www.windermeregolfclub.co.uk
Email: office@windermeregc.co.uk
Telephone: +44 (0) 15394 43123

Par: 67 / 70 (Red)
Length: 4,548yds-5,122yds
Type: Parkland

Fees:
● per round

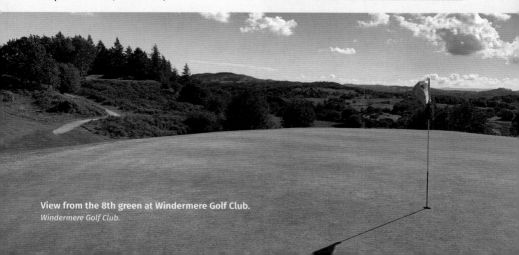

View from the 8th green at Windermere Golf Club.
Windermere Golf Club.

Yorkshire

GANTON GOLF CLUB

Ganton,
Nr Scarborough,
North Yorkshire,
YO12 4PA
www.gantongolfclub.com
Phone: +44 (0) 1944 710329
Email: secretary@gantongolfclub.com

General course information –
Par: 71,72 (Blue) / 73 (White) /
72 (Yellow) / 76 (Red)

S.S.S: 75 (Blue) / 74 (White) /
72 (Yellow) / 77 (Red)

Slope rating: 138 (Blue/White) / 133
(Yellow) / 145 (Red)

Length: 6,063yds–7,016yds

Longest hole: Par-5 13th, 468yds–565yds

Shortest hole: Par-3 5th, 150yds–159yds
(Par-3 10th, 132 yds, red tees)

Type: Inland Links

Handicap Certificate: Required
(maximum handicap is 28 for men
and 36 for ladies)

Green fees:
(Low season)
● per round / per day (Weekday /
Weekends & Bank Holidays)

(Shoulder season)
● per round / ● per day (Weekday)
● per round / per day
(Weekend & Bank Holidays)

(High season)
● per round / per day (Weekday)
● per round / ● per day
(Weekend & Bank Holidays)

Twilight rate:
● per round (after 4 pm)

Caddies: A limited number
available. (Booking in advance via
caddiemaster +44 (0) 1944 712804).

Equipment hire:
Buggies available on medical
grounds (personal buggies not
allowed). Clubs and trolleys can be
hired from the pro shop in advance
on +44 (0) 1944 710260.

How do I book a round of golf?
Ganton welcomes visitors to apply
for a tee-time during the week.
There are no tee-times available on
Saturday mornings.
    There are three ways to book a
round of golf at Ganton Golf Club:

Online:
www.gantongolfclub.com/Visitors/
Green fees

Price Guide: ● up to £49 | ● £50 – £99 | ● £100 – £149 | ● £150 – £200 | ● over £200

Phone:
+44 (0) 1944 710329

Email:
secretary@gantongolfclub.com /
gary@gantongolfclub.com

HISTORY

Originally formed as The Scarborough Golf Club in 1891 by a group of gentlemen who both lived locally or chose to holiday in the fashionable spa town. The family of Sir Charles Legard Bart, one of the founding members, owned the Ganton estate, ten miles inland from Scarborough. Sir Charles recommended a patch of land adjacent to Ganton Village as a suitable site for a golf course. Sixteen years later, the name was changed to Ganton Golf Club.

The development of golf courses at this time coincided with the expansion of the railway around Great Britain and Ganton was no exception. Many members travelled to the course by train, where they were met by their caddies who would then accompany them on the short walk between Ganton Station and the clubhouse. At the end of each day, 10 minutes before the last train was due, a bell would ring both inside and outside the clubhouse, prompting members to make their way back to the station for their journey home.

Tom Chisholm of St Andrews, assisted by Robert Bird (who would become the club's first professional and green keeper), designed the initial course layout. Following Bird's departure, the resident professionals at Ganton read as a veritable who's who of golf's finest players of the era.

Harry Vardon won three of his six Open Championships during his spell at the club (1896–1903), followed by Ted Ray (1903–12) who would go on to win both The Open (1912) and US Open (1920) during his career.

Ganton's first major redesign in 1905 was a combined effort by the great triumvirate – James Braid, John Henry Taylor and Harry Vardon. Other architects who have left their mark on the course are Harry Colt (1907, 1911 and 1931), Dr Alister MacKenzie (1912 and 1920), Tom Simpson (1934) and C.K. Cotton (1948 and 1952).

Throughout its history, Ganton has played host to some of golf's most prestigious tournaments. Its proudest achievement is unquestionably as one of only four clubs (along with Royal Lytham, Royal Birkdale and The Honourable Company of Edinburgh Golfers – Muirfield), to hold the

The 18th green sits in front of Ganton's splendid clubhouse. *kevinmurraygolfphotography.com*

distinction of being host venue for The Ryder Cup (1949), The Curtis Cup (2000) and The Walker Cup (2003).

When considering which clubs have assisted the development of the modern game across the British Isles, both professional and amateur, there's no doubt Ganton can lay a strong claim for a seat at the top table.

PLAYING THE COURSE

If The Open Championship were ever to venture away from the coastline, it's hard to imagine a more appropriate location than here. Ganton is a very special place to play golf.

Surrounded by some of Yorkshire's most picturesque countryside, Ganton resides in a serene setting, oozing effortless style and an unashamedly old fashioned golfing experience from the moment you arrive.

Arguably the UK's finest example of a genuine inland links layout, Ganton's springy, sand-based terrain and fast, gently undulating fairways coupled with vast, cavernous bunkers provide a stern test from tee to green. Nothing less than straight down the middle is essential for a good score here.

The opening three holes, all medium-length par-4s, offer a fairly gentle start allowing you to warm up your swing ahead of the more rigorous challenges that lay ahead. The 1st fairway, slightly uphill from the tee, is quite generous and allows enough space for any wayward drives to avoid bunkers on either side. Your approach can afford to be either short or long towards a green sloping back to front but must avoid two steep bunkers both left and right.

After the slight right-to-left dogleg 2nd, hole 3 – at 349yds from the back tees – is the first driveable par-4. The safe line is more toward the right-hand side of the fairway. If you're going for the green, beware the two bunkers along this side ready to catch anything pushed too far wide.

The stretch of holes from the 4th through to the 7th is the real standout section on the front-9. The 4th is a fabulous par-4 links hole. Aim your tee shot along the left side of the fairway to leave the best line in for your approach over the valley towards the raised plateau green. The putting surface slopes back to front so anything short risks rolling back down the slope.

The 5th is a fairly short but tricky par-3 (the first of only three on the course). The green sits downhill with plenty of room to aim for from the raised tee, however, anything missing could well find sand among the four bunkers surrounding it.

The 6th is a pretty straight, slightly uphill, par-5 (par-4 from the back tees) requiring a straight tee-shot needing to thread its way between two large fairway bunkers both left and right. Long hitters can reach in two, however, there are plenty more sand hazards surrounding the area approaching the green ready to catch any shots landing left or right.

Hole 7 is a long, dogleg right, par-4 and the hardest on the course. Your tee-shot needs to land on the left side of the fairway for the best line toward the putting surface, sitting uphill. Your approach is also best aimed left in order to feed down the two-tiered green toward the pin.

The back-9 starts with another testing par-3 requiring an accurate mid-iron shot. Anything pushed right may find one of three pot bunkers along that side. Only straight at the centre will do if you're to secure your par.

The 12th is another sharp, dogleg right, par-4. Your tee-shot needs to wrap around the pine tree on the right of the fairway to leave a relatively straightforward approach into a heavily contoured green.

The driveable par-4 14th green with the village church steeple in the background.
kevinmurraygolfphotography.com

(15) **SIGNATURE HOLE: PAR-4 15TH, 420YDS–493YDS.**

After a classic, short, risk/reward par-4 at the 14th (anything other than straight and long will find trouble if you go for it), you reach the hardest hole on the back-9. A long, straight par-4 needing two perfectly struck shots to get anywhere close to a difficult, two-tiered green.

A huge bunker along the left of the fairway shouldn't really come into play for the longer hitters off the tee. Shorter hitters may be smarter using a three-shot strategy to reach the putting surface. Keep it straight all the way and you'll be fine. On or around par at this hole is a very good score.

Hole 16 is a long downhill par-4 with the small matter of traversing the largest bunker on the course, stretching across the fairway, from the tee. At just over 180yds to clear, it really shouldn't come into play. Just make sure your tee-shot is straight and true and you'll be fine.

The 17th is another popular hole, playing either as a (very) long par-3 or a short par-4 (251yds from the back tees), across the access road into

Looking back down the 16th fairway from behind the green.
kevinmurraygolfphotography.com

the property. There's plenty to aim for and lots of space at the front of the green if you fall short with your drive.

Finally, the 18th brings you back in the opposite direction. Your tee-shot is blind over a large waste sand area called 'The Pandy'. Aim slightly right of the marker for the perfect landing point on the fairway. From here you have a clear shot back across the road toward the green.

18-hole courses nearby

● SCARBOROUGH NORTH CLIFF GOLF CLUB

The present course dates back to 1928 and was originally designed by James Braid. The layout begins on the cliff tops before moving inland and finishes back at the cliffs offering spectacular views out towards Scarborough Castle.

Website: www.northcliffgolfclub.co.uk
Email: info@northcliffgolfclub.co.uk
Telephone: +44 (0) 1723 355397

Par: 72 (White/Yellow) / 73 (Red)
Length: 5,595yds–6,493yds
Type: Parkland

Fees:
● per round (weekdays & weekends)

● SCARBOROUGH SOUTH CLIFF GOLF CLUB

Originally formed at the beginning of the last century. The course was neglected during the First World War before Dr Alister MacKenzie was commissioned to resurrect the site, which is, with some alterations due to land erosion, the one that is played today.

Website: www.southcliffgolfclub.com
Email: clubsecretary@ southcliffgolfclub.com
Telephone: +44 (0) 1723 360522

Par: 72
Length: 5,506yds–6,432yds
Type: Parkland

Fees:
● per round (weekdays & weekends)

THE ALWOODLEY GOLF CLUB

Wigton Lane,
Leeds,
LS17 8SA
www.alwoodley.co.uk
Phone: +44 (0) 113 268 1680
Email: manager@alwoodley.co.uk

General course information –
Par: 71 (Blue) / 72 (White) / 70 (Yellow) / 73 (Red)

S.S.S: 74 (Blue) / 73 (White) / 71 (Yellow) / 74 (Red)

Slope rating: 138 (Blue) / 136 (White) / 130 (Yellow) / 135 (Red)

Length: 5,579yds–6,914yds

Longest hole: Par-5 8th, 456yds–591yds

Shortest hole: Par-3 7th, 128yds–141yds

Type: Heathland

(Blue tees typically used by members and for championships, white tees recommended for single-digit handicappers, yellow and red recommended for double-digit handicappers)

Handicap Certificate: Not required

Green fees:
(Low season)
● per round (Weekdays & Sundays)

(Shoulder season)
● per round / ● per day
(Weekdays & Sundays)

(High season)
● per round / ● per day
(Weekdays & Sundays)

Caddies: May be available upon specific request (must be booked in advance)

Equipment hire:
Clubs, buggies* and trolleys can be hired from the pro shop.
(*available if required on medical grounds with appropriate certificate)

How do I book a round of golf?
Alwoodley welcomes visitors at all times from Sunday-Friday to play the course.
    There are two ways to book a round of golf at The Alwoodley Golf Club:

Phone:
+44 (0) 113 268 1680 or +44 (0) 113 268 9603

Email:
manager@alwoodley.co.uk

Price Guide: ● up to £49 | ● £50 – £99 | ● £100 – £149 | ● £150 – £200 | ● over £200

HISTORY

Cypress Point and Augusta National; two golf courses with many common traits. They both fight it out atop most respected golf publications' lists for the best and most aesthetically pleasing courses you'll find anywhere in the world. Cypress Point's 16th and Augusta's 13th are considered, arguably, to be the finest golf holes ever created. These fabled courses also share something in common with Alwoodley – their original designer, Dr Alister MacKenzie.

Born to Scottish parents in Normanton on the outskirts of Leeds, MacKenzie spent his formative adult years at his father's medical practice. A keen golfer throughout this time, in 1907 Alister would become one of the founder members of the newly formed Alwoodley Golf Club.

Influenced by his service during the Boer War some years earlier (as part of a unit responsible for advising the army on camouflage techniques), MacKenzie would cut his course design teeth at Alwoodley. Other than the length, the current layout is pretty much as it was when originally created. The MacKenzie hallmarks of variety and strategy set among a natural heathland landscape are all as evident today as they were over a hundred years ago.

1st green surrounded by gorse bushes at the back with the 2nd hole beyond. *David Cannon/Getty Images*

Dr MacKenzie would go on to international acclaim designing courses all over the world, but it is here at Alwoodley, his home course, where he took his first steps on the road to becoming one of the finest course architects of all time.

Today the course is a regular host venue for R&A, England Golf and Yorkshire Union events. In 2019 Alwoodley hosted The Brabazon Trophy for the first time, one of the world's premier amateur stroke play competitions, which saw 16-year-old Ben Schmidt triumph as the youngest ever winner of the tournament.

PLAYING THE COURSE

One of the most intriguing aspects of playing a round of golf at Alwoodley, because of what we know about the connection between this course and the one in Georgia, is that you get to wonder which holes may have influenced Dr MacKenzie's thinking as he mapped out his designs for Augusta National.

Set right in the heart of a cluster of MacKenzie-designed courses, Alwoodley is a terrific heathland challenge with tight, fast fairways leading towards large, undulating, greens. The good doctor knew a thing or two about clever bunker positions and it was here where he honed his craft. Recent work, completed by Ken Moodie, has seen almost all of the bunkers restored to their original specifications.

At Alwoodley you don't need to be a big hitter to secure a good score but it does pay to keep it straight. Any stray shots from the tee into the heather or surrounding woodland can punish your scorecard and put pressure on your recovery game. Be solid rather than bold from the tee and you'll enjoy your round a lot more.

Any seasoned Alwoodley member will tell you that the first twelve holes provide the best chance of getting a good score, as they generally tend to play with the prevailing wind behind you. Don't leave yourself playing catch up against your playing partners by the time you reach the 13th or the drinks will likely be on you in the clubhouse.

Hole 1 is a good opening par-4 with a wide, generous, fairway toward a large green that slopes back to front. Aim your drive toward the left to give yourself the best angle for your approach onto the green. Be careful not to aim too long with your approach as large gorse bushes surround the back of the green.

Before you leave the 1st green for the 2nd hole, take a look a hundred yards to your right and make a mental note for later of the pin position on the 17th green as your second shot on this hole is blind.

The 3rd is the first par-5 (there are only two from the yellow tees – both on the front-9 – and five from the red tees) and starts with a demanding tee-shot tempting you toward the left of the fairway where two large bunkers wait to catch your ball. Your approach must navigate a pot bunker on the right toward a green with a steep 'MacKenzie' style slope in the middle from right to left.

The view from the par-4 5th tee offers a wonderful panorama of the course so take a moment to admire your surroundings. Your tee shot here needs to stay left to allow the ball to follow the severe slope on the fairway. The raised green can make the pin hard to spot and is well guarded by bunkers at the front.

(8) SIGNATURE HOLE: PAR-5 8TH, 456YDS–591YDS.

If there is one hole that best represents everything that is great about the course at Alwoodley, it is this one. The par-5 8th is not just one of the prettiest but also the longest and toughest hole on the course. Try not to let its appearance distract you. With out of bounds on the left and deep rough on the right, an accurate drive from the tee is essential.

A decision must be made with your second shot with a large bunker and a lip of rough lying 140yds from the green. Do you lay up or go for it? Once you navigate the fairway, you reach a tiered green with three different levels. A par here should be cherished.

The 10th hole is steeped in MacKenzie legend and provided the inspiration for Augusta's 13th (Azalea). When you stand on the tee box and look out at the fairway swinging sharply from right to left on the crest of a hill, it's nigh on impossible not to make the comparison (akin to seeing an early sketched version of the Mona Lisa). Big hitters can make the green in two if they land at the top of the hill, but trouble lurks on either side, all the way to the green.

Hole 11 is a memorable par-3 and many members' favourite. This hole is all about the green, which slopes severely from right to left. Short and right is a good miss but anything left could be in big trouble. Once on the putting surface you may have to aim at right angles to get your ball near the hole.

The tough closing stretch starts at the 13th consisting of mid to long par-4s and a long par-3 at the 14th. Holes 16 and 18 are par-5s from the red tees. The 15th is a rare left-to-right dogleg toward a sloping green, well protected by bunkers front left and right – hitting the left side of the green is a must here.

View of the 11th green from the tee-box. *David Cannon/Getty Images*

The 18th fairway, guarded by bunkers on both sides and the clubhouse in the background.
David Cannon/Getty Images

Don't be fooled by the 16th's appearance from the tee – there's more room to the right than there looks upon first glance so aim in that direction to avoid fairway bunkers on the left.

Many regard the 18th as the best closing hole in Yorkshire. The 'hog's-back' fairway makes for an extremely tricky drive as it can throw what appears to be a perfect shot off line into one of many bunkers lining up both left and right all the way to the green.

18-hole courses nearby

● **MOOR ALLERTON GOLF CLUB**
The club relocated to its current site in 1971. The course is the only UK layout designed by renowned architect, Robert Trent Jones. In all there are twenty-seven holes with three distinct loops of nine, blending in beautifully against the surrounding landscape.

Website: www.moorallertongolfclub.co.uk
Email: info@magc.co.uk
Telephone: +44 (0) 113 266 1154

Par: 36 (Lakes) / 35 (Blackmoor) / 36 (High)
Length: 3,319yds (Lakes) / 3,151yds (Blackmoor) / 3,522yds (High)
Type: Parkland

Fees:
● per round (18 holes)

● **LEEDS GOLF CENTRE – WIKE RIDGE**
Great facility, open to golfers of all ages. In addition to the 18-hole course there's also a number of other attractions including a 12-hole par-3 course and a Leadbetter Golf Academy.

Website: www.leedsgolfcentre.com
Email: info@leedsgolfcentre.com
Telephone: +44 (0) 113 288 6000

Par: 72
Length: 5,472yds–6,535yds
Type: Woodland

Fees:
● per round (Weekdays / Weekends & Bank Holidays)

MOORTOWN GOLF CLUB

Harrogate Road,
Alwoodley,
Leeds,
LS17 7DB
www.moortown-gc.co.uk
Phone: +44 (0) 113 268 6521
Email: secretary@moortown-gc.co.uk

General course information –
Par: 71 (Blue/White/Yellow) / 75 (Red)

S.S.S: 74 (Blue) 73 (White) 72 (Yellow)
75 (Red)

Slope rating: 141 (Blue) / 140 (White) /
133 (Yellow) / 146 (Red)

Length: 5,939yds–6,980yds

Longest hole: Par-5 12th,
509yds–554yds

Shortest hole: Par-3 17th 122yds–155yds
(Par-3 4th & 10th 175yds from blue
tees)

Type: Heathland

Handicap Certificate: Not required

Green fees:
(Low season)
● per round

(Shoulder season)
● per round

(High season)
● per round

Junior rates:
50 per cent of regular green fee

Twilight rate:
● per round (after 4pm)

Caddies: Available upon specific
request (must be booked in
advance).

Equipment hire:
Clubs, buggies and trolleys can be
hired from the pro shop.

How do I book a round of golf?
Moortown welcomes visitors at all
times during the week – including
weekends – to play its course.
(No tee-times available for visitors
until after 2.30 pm on Saturdays)
   There are three ways to book a
round of golf at Moortown Golf Club:

Online:
www.moortown-gc.co.uk/Visitors/
Green Fees

Phone:
+44 (0) 113 268 6521

Email:
secretary@moortown-gc.co.uk

Price Guide: ● up to £49 | ● £50 – £99 | ● £100 – £149 | ● £150 – £200 | ● over £200

HISTORY

A holiday to the seaside town of Bridlington on the east coast of Yorkshire by Fred Lawson-Brown in 1903 would provide the backdrop for the formation of Moortown Golf Club. While there, Fred decided to spend a day watching the Yorkshire Amateur Golf Championships taking place twenty miles up the road at Ganton.

The exquisite setting for which the golf course at Ganton was (and still is) renowned, captivated Lawson-Brown so much that he became entranced with the idea that his home town of Leeds really should have one of these too. After much deliberation and searching for the right area, Moortown Golf Club was formed in 1909 using a piece of land on the Bramham Estate, just north of the city centre.

Dr Alister MacKenzie, fresh from his work across the road at Alwoodley, was recruited for only his second design assignment. MacKenzie would later become famous as the designer of such acclaimed sites as Cypress Point, Royal Melbourne and, of course, Augusta National.

Moortown's opening was a truly grand affair (delayed due to the death of King Edward VII) in September 1910 with an exhibition match between the reigning Open Champion, James Braid and another member of the great triumvirate, Harry Vardon. Moortown could not have chosen two more esteemed golfers at the time to celebrate its inauguration.

View from the 1st tee at dusk. *Moortown Golf Club*

However, it would be as host venue of a new international tournament between Great Britain and the USA, held on these shores for the first time, in 1929 as a piece of history for which Moortown is most proud of – the Ryder Cup.

The largest crowd ever to attend a golf tournament in the UK at the time descended on Moortown to witness the greats of the game duel over two days in what became known as 'The Battle of the Moor'. At the end, the GB team, led by George Duncan, would emerge triumphant by a score of 7–5 versus a US team including such greats as Gene Sarazon and Walter Hagen (US captain). Both Hagen and Duncan would later become honorary members of Moortown.

For their organisational help and support during the tournament, the ladies section of the club were awarded their own trophy by Samuel Ryder – The Ryder Commemoration Cup – which is still proudly played for each year by the lady members.

PLAYING THE COURSE

Five miles outside Leeds city centre and just across the road from its older MacKenzie-designed neighbour, Moortown is an imposing test of golf laid out in splendid, natural heathland surroundings. The classic MacKenzie hallmarks – large, undulating greens and clever bunker positioning – are evident all around the course, as is his love of memorable short holes.

As nature took its course over the decades and enveloped the environment, Moortown resembled more of a Parkland layout, particularly

Aerial view of the 6th, 9th and 10th holes at Moortown. *Moortown Golf Club*

between the 1970s through to the 1990s. An extensive maintenance programme from the start of this century has stripped back large swathes of trees returning the course to its original heathland habitat.

From a total of ninety-six bunkers on the course, twenty-four were uncovered during the recent renovations, following a review of the original mapping used by MacKenzie, which had become hidden when regular course maintenance was abandoned for long periods during the Second World War.

The longer holes here are not quite as wide as they seem from the tee-boxes, so an emphasis on keeping straight off the tee is key if you want to avoid the many heather beds or tree clusters bordering the fairways.

The round starts with a short par-5 (488yds from the back tees, 454yds from the front). The fairway slopes down from the tee-box and is pretty well guarded on either side. The green is fairly flat, but your approach needs to thread its way past bunkers at the front, both right and left.

After two par-4s, the 4th is the first short hole. It is called 'Spinney' and you will see why when you reach the tee-box as clusters of trees surround three sides of the green. A solid tee-shot (either a four or five-iron is recommended) is needed to make it beyond three bunkers lurking at the front of the putting surface.

Holes 6 and 7 are relatively new holes, introduced in 1989. The 6th is a long par-4 and represents a real heathland feel true to MacKenzie's original design. The par-5 7th places a premium on accuracy both from the tee and fairway to avoid falling foul of any fairway bunkers or the water hazard running along the left-hand side.

10 **SIGNATURE HOLE: PAR-3 10TH, 145YDS–175YDS, 'GIBRALTAR'.**
Dr MacKenzie's masterpiece and used as his prototype hole before construction commenced on the rest of the course.

Often compared to the Redan at North Berwick although MacKenzie would deny ever seeing the Redan hole before he designed this one. Your tee-shot is aimed towards a heavily contoured green sat atop a raised plateau. Any imperfect shot can expect to be scooped up by one of the bunkers positioned around the putting surface. Anything beyond the pin will likely be lost so aim right at the heart of the green.

The par-5 12th is the longest hole on the course. A patch of bunkered cross rough 280yds from the tee adds extra spice to your drive. Do you go for it or lay up? In over 100 years of history, only one albatross has ever been recorded here.

After the long 12th, four testing par-4s follow on the demanding closing stretch before the final par-3 at the 17th. Here your tee-shot has to contend with a large bunker on the left and two on the right, protecting a green which slopes up from the front. Anything from a short iron to a wood may be needed depending on the conditions.

From the 18th tee you can see the clubhouse out in front of you. At this final par-4, aim slightly left with your drive to leave the best line with your approach towards a large green well protected by bunkers at the front and gorse bushes at the back.

The 10th green, protected by a large bunker at the front - MacKenzie's Redan hole.
kevinmurraygolfphotography.com

18-hole courses nearby

● HEADINGLEY GOLF CLUB

Founded in October 1892 and set in an exquisite rural location, Headingley is the oldest golf club in Leeds. Both Alister MacKenzie and Harry Colt have overseen redesigns to the course. Henry Cotton described the par-3 17th here as one of the finest short holes he's ever played.

Website: www.headingleygolfclub.co.uk
Email: manager@headingleygolfclub.co.uk
Phone: +44 (0) 113 267 9573

Par: 71 (White / Yellow / Blue) / 74 (Red)
Length: 5,515yds–6,575yds
Type: Heathland / Moorland / Parkland

Fees:
● per round / day

● SAND MOOR GOLF CLUB

Opened in 1926 and offering lovely views over Eccup reservoir. Originally designed by Dr MacKenzie who also sat on the first Club Greens committee. Re-designed in the 1960s, the collection of par-3s are considered a real highlight of the course.

Website: www.sandmoorgolf.co.uk
Email: info@sandmoorgolf.co.uk
Telephone: +44 (0) 113 268 5180

Par: 71 (White / Yellow) / 73 (Red)
Length: 5,584yds–6,446yds
Type: Inland

Fees:
● per round (Mon-Fri / Sundays & Bank Holidays)

Other courses in the area

Below is a further selection of wonderful courses in Yorkshire well worth seeking out if you're in the area.

● LINDRICK GOLF CLUB

Host course for the 1957 Ryder Cup and scene of the last ever victory for a GB&I team (and, at the time, their first for twenty-four years). Lindrick also hosted the 1960 Curtis Cup. The course provides a mix of both heathland and moorland charm, noted for its firm, fast greens.

Website: www.lindrickgolfclub.co.uk
Email: info@lindrickgolfclub.co.uk
Telephone: +44 (0) 1909 475282

Par: 70 (Blue) / 75 (Red)
Length: 5,772yds–6,665yds
Type: Heathland / Moorland

Fees:
● per round* / ● per day*
(* = available Monday – Friday)

DEWSBURY DISTRICT GOLF CLUB

Formed in October 1891. The course lies on a steep hillside, offering fabulous views of the surrounding countryside and was originally designed as a 9-hole course by Old Tom Morris. The layout was expanded to 18 holes by Ted Ray in 1906 and has received further alterations by both Peter Alliss and Dave Thomas in the early 1970s.

Website: www.dewsburygolf.co.uk
Email: info@dewsburygolf.co.uk
Telephone: +44 (0) 1924 492399

Par: 71 / 74 (Red)
Length: 5,717yds–6,360yds
Type: Parkland

Fees:
● (day ticket)

PANNAL GOLF CLUB

One of Yorkshire's finest examples of a moorland course, sat on quite high ground and can prove to be particularly challenging when the wind is blowing. Both MacKenzie brothers (Alister and Charles) were involved in redesigns of the course at separate times.

Website: www.pannalgc.co.uk
Email: office@pannalgc.co.uk
Phone: +44 (0) 1423 872628

Par: 72 / 74 (Red)
Length: 5,848yds–6,404yds
Type: Moorland

Fees:
● per round (weekdays & weekends)

HUDDERSFIELD GOLF CLUB

Known by members and regular visitors as Fixby Hall. Founded in 1891, the original course was designed by Tom Dunn and the first club professional was Alex Herd (when he was just 23 years old). Eleven years later Herd would win The Open Championship at Hoylake (1902).

Website: www.huddersfield-golf.
co.uk
Email: gm@huddersfield-golf.co.uk
Telephone: +44 (0) 1484 426203

Par: 71 / 73 (Red)
Length: 5,595yds–6,499yds
Type: Moorland/Parkland

Fees:
● per round (low season)
● per round (high season)

CLEVELAND GOLF CLUB

Formed in 1887, therefore, the oldest golf club in Yorkshire. Many fine architects, including Old Tom Morris, Harry Colt and more recently, Donald Steel have had a hand in the design of this grand old links course. A true test of seaside golf, particularly when the wind blows.

Website: www.cleveland-golf-club.com
Email: majuba@btconnect.com
Telephone: +44 (0) 1642 471798

Par: 72
Length: 5,545yds–6,921yds
Type: Links

Fees:
● per round

● **CROW NEST PARK GOLF CLUB (9 HOLES)**

Opened in 1995 and set within a beautiful parkland environment. One of the finest examples of a 9-hole course you will find in the UK. Alternative tees are available for 18-hole rounds.

Website: www.crownestgolf.co.uk
Email: info@crownestgolf.co.uk
Phone: +44 (0) 1484 401152

Par: 35 / 36 (Red)
Length: 2,771yds–3,054yds
Type: Parkland

Fees:
£9.00 (9 holes)
£16.00 (18 holes)

● **HEBDEN BRIDGE GOLF CLUB (9 HOLES)**

A real hidden gem set high on a hillside among the West Yorkshire Pennines, overlooking Hebden Bridge. This course, on a clear day, provides views that are hard to match – anywhere.

Website: www.hebdenbridgegolfclub. co.uk

Email: N/A
Phone: +44 (0) 1422 842896

Par: 34 / 35 (Red)
Length: 2,420yds–2,582yds
Type: Moorland

Fees:
£10.00* (9 holes)
£15.00* (18 holes)
* = honesty box in operation

● **TODMORDEN GOLF CLUB (9 HOLES)**

Originally opened in 1905 and set on a plateau above the peaceful village of Todmorden. This extremely picturesque 9-hole course provides a real challenge with narrow fairways surrounded by thick rough.

Website: www.todmordengolfclub. co.uk
Email: secretary@ todmordengolfclub.co.uk
Phone: +44 (0) 1706 812986

Par: 34
Length: 2,463yds–2,951yds
Type: Moorland

Fees:
£10.00 (9 holes)

North West – England's Golf Coast

ROYAL LYTHAM & ST ANNES GOLF CLUB

Links Gate,
Lytham St Annes,
Lancashire
FY8 3LQ
www.royallytham.org
Phone: +44 (0) 1253 724206
Email: bookings@royallytham.org

General course information –
Par: 71 (Red/Green) / 75 (Orange)

S.S.S: 74 (Red) / 72 (Green) / 75 (Orange)

Slope rating: 143 (Red) / 135 (Green) / 143 (Orange)

Length: 5,854yds–6,731yds

Longest hole: Par-5 7th, 512yds–569yds

Shortest hole: Par-3 9th, 137yds–156yds

Type: Links

Handicap Certificate: Not required

Green fees:
(Low season)
● per round

(Shoulder season)
● per round

(High season)
● per round

Junior rates: 50 per cent of regular green fee

Caddies:
£50 per player per round (paid in cash + gratuity). Limited availability and must be booked well in advance via the pro shop, +44 (0) 1253 724206.

Equipment hire:
Two buggies available if required on medical grounds and pull trolleys can be hired from the pro shop.

How do I book a round of golf?
Royal Lytham & St Annes welcomes visitors to play the championship course at the following times during the week:

Monday:	10.10 am–12.30 pm and from 2.40 pm–4.00 pm
Thursday:	8.40 am–1.50 pm and from 2.40 pm–4.00 pm
Tuesday, Wednesday, Friday, Saturday and Sunday:	2.40 pm–4.00 pm

Price Guide: ● up to £49 | ● £50 – £99 | ● £100 – £149 | ● £150 – £200 | ● over £200

For Dormy House guests the following tee-times are reserved each day:
8.00 am–8.30 am and 2.00 pm–2.30 pm (these times may vary at the weekend).

There are three ways to book a round of golf at Royal Lytham & St Annes Golf Club:

Online:
www.royallytham.org/Visitor Online Booking

Phone:
Via the bookings department, +44 (0) 1253 724206

Email:
bookings@royallytham.org

HISTORY

Formed in 1886, The Lytham & St Annes Golf Club originally played at St Annes Old Links Course before moving to its present site in 1897. Local professional George Lowe designed the course initially. Since Lowe's efforts, an assortment of distinguished architects have left their mark on the layout: Herbert Fowler, Tom Simpson, C.K Cotton and, most famously, Harry Colt, who orchestrated a major remodelling of the course in the 1920s.

Throughout its illustrious history, Royal Lytham has played host to many of golf's most esteemed competitions including The Walker Cup (2015, won by Great Britain & Ireland), The Women's British Open (five times overall, most recently in 2018, won by Georgia Hall), The Ryder Cup (1961 and 1977, won on both occasions by USA) and, of course, The Open Championship on eleven occasions.

The club received its 'Royal' patronage from George V just in time to host its first Open in 1926. The 61st edition is famous as the first of three triumphs for US amateur Bobby Jones. It is particularly remembered for what is described as one of the greatest recovery shots ever produced to win a Championship.

Languishing in hard sand off the 17th fairway with no view of the putting surface and his opponent, Al Watrous, on the green in two, Jones produced an incredible approach shot using his mashie club (5-iron in old currency) to land inside Watrous' ball. Astounded by the majesty of his opponent's effort, Watrous 3-putted, handing Jones the initiative with only the 18th hole remaining.

The fairway at the par-4 8th hole sits below the green leaving a tough approach shot.
Royal Lytham & St Annes Golf Club

After his win Jones gave his mashie club to a journalist who, in turn, handed it to Royal Lytham where it still proudly resides to this day. The 'Bobby Jones Iron' is an annual club competition, played since 1955 in honour of Jones' achievement.

Other exalted Open winners at Royal Lytham include Seve Ballesteros, who won two of his three titles at this venue in 1979 and 1988. Most famously, in 1979 at just 22 years of age, during the closing stretch of the final round, Seve hit his tee-shot at the 16th into an overflow car park and was granted a free drop from where he pitched onto the green and dropped a monster putt for a birdie.

2019 also saw the return of The Senior Open Championship to Royal Lytham, for the fifth time, with a victory for Bernhard Langer (his fourth title overall).

PLAYING THE COURSE

By its own admission, this grand old master lacks one rather obvious characteristic shared by all other venues on The Open rota that hug the coastline. Nevertheless Royal Lytham's suburban setting has an intrinsic charm all of its own. Sea view or no sea view, you'll remember your round of golf at this majestic links course for a very long time.

If you're searching for a constant examination of how straight you can hit a golf ball then look no further. A badly sliced tee shot won't find the shoreline, but it could quite easily discover rail tracks or one of 184 bunkers so ingeniously plotted around the fairways.

With the exception of a handful of holes (specifically 6, 8 and 10) this is a relatively flat course for a links, largely devoid of the usual undulating rollercoaster fairways. The great courses don't try and hide anything, they're happy to show you the way, but leave getting there up to you.

The 1st hole provides an immediate test, so be sure you've hit a few practice balls before you get to the tee. The green at this long, par-3 opening hole is extremely well protected by five bunkers at the front, ready to gobble up any nervy first tee shots that don't quite carry.

Despite the lack of sea views, holes 2 and 3 offer you the first glimpse of a familiar feature intertwined with all great links courses, albeit one it's best to steer clear from – a railway line.

The tracks run along the right-hand side of each of these par-4s. Both holes tempt you to flirt with out of bounds by offering a better line into the green from the right side of the fairway. A cluster of bunkers wait menacingly along the left to draw in any wayward tee-shot.

The 6th hole is the first of two back-to-back par-5s and, at 494yds from the red tees, offers an opportunity to claw back any dropped shots to this point. However, a severely undulating fairway offers strong protection along with three bunkers guarding the front of a slightly crowned green.

The second par-5 at hole 7 is much longer (569yds from the red tees), flanked along each side of a narrow fairway by bunkers, mounds and thick rough. The raised green, while not heavily bunkered, slopes away from you making your approach shot tricky to place.

Hole 8 brings the railway line back into play, again along the right. Dead ground between three cross-bunkers and the raised green, along with the deepest bunker on the course sitting left of the putting surface, make this one of the toughest holes on the course.

The heavily bunkered par-3 9th hole, despite being the shortest on the course, leaves you with no other option except landing your ball right in the centre of the green. Your tee-shot at the par-4 10th is blind and needs to thread its way through the narrow gap between mounds either side of the marker post, showing you the line to aim for.

The 10th green protected by pot bunkers at the front. *Royal Lytham & St Annes Golf Club*

The 11th is the longest hole on the course and typically plays into the wind making this par-5 a genuine 3-shot towards a raised, undulating green. Try and keep left here off the tee for the best line in with your approach.

The final three holes at Royal Lytham have all provided the stage for some of The Open Championship's most unforgettable moments.

The 16th, a relatively short par-4, is steeped in Open folklore thanks to a nearby overflow car park and the brilliance of a certain Spanish golfing legend. Your tee-shot is blind, but try not to go too far right as not many among us mere mortals have shots in our armoury to match Seve's astonishing effort onto the green in '79. Play it safe.

View from the 18th tee looking straight down the fairway towards the clubhouse.
Royal Lytham & St Annes Golf Club

(17) SIGNATURE HOLE: PAR-4 17TH (PAR-5 FROM ORANGE TEES), 404YDS–432YDS.

From the site of where a young Ballesteros announced himself upon the golfing world, on to one that bore witness to a golf shot so great they placed a plaque on the exact spot where it was taken. The par-4 17th, swarmed by bunkers either side and across, is a tough dogleg left towards an open green.

The Bobby Jones plaque lies on the left of the fairway by the third drive bunker and commemorates his terrific effort which secured the 1926 Open Championship – don't miss it.

Finally to the 18th, and a classic finishing hole; mid-range, straight, par-4 with two lines of fairway bunkers ready to catch your tee-shot and the green (the longest on the course) sat in the shadow of the clubhouse.

Tony Jacklin stood on the 18th tee in 1969, nerves jangling having just dropped a shot at the 17th, and with the great Bob Charles breathing down his neck. Managing to steady himself, Jacklin unleashed a drive that was perfectly described by golf commentator, Henry Longhurst, at the time – 'Oh, what a corker!' And the rest is history.

A relentless demand upon shot accuracy towards greens that are firm, fast and true form the basis of why Royal Lytham rightly occupies a regular place among the finest, most challenging, courses you will find in the British Isles.

18-hole courses nearby

● ST ANNES OLD LINKS GOLF CLUB

Founded in 1901, this highly regarded links course was a favourite of the great Bobby Jones. The signature 9th hole here has previously been voted one of the best in the UK.

Website: www.stannesoldlinks.com
Email: secretary@stannesoldlinks.com
Telephone: +44 (0) 1253 723597

Par: 72
Length: 5,610yds–6,941yds
Type: Links

Fees:
● per round
(Members only on Saturdays)

● FAIRHAVEN GOLF CLUB

Originally a 12-hole course prior to a redesign in 1924 by James Braid and J.H. Steer. A fine course with over 100 bunkers offering a stern test for golfers of all abilities.

Website: www.fairhavengolfclub.co.uk
Email: secretary@fairhavengolfclub.co.uk
Telephone: +44 (0) 1253 736741

Par: 72 (Blue) / 75 (Red)
Length: 5,991yds–6,950yds
Type: Links

Fees:
● per round

● LYTHAM GREEN DRIVE GOLF CLUB

Founded in 1913, this pleasant parkland course has previously hosted final Open qualifying and has a well-earned reputation for offering a warm welcome to all its visitors.

Website: www.lythamgreendrive.co.uk
Email: secretary@lythamgreendrive.co.uk
Telephone: +44 (0) 1253 737390

Par: 70 (White) / 74 (Red)
Length: 5,762yds–6,309yds
Type: Parkland

Fees:
● per round

6

ROYAL BIRKDALE GOLF CLUB

Waterloo Road,
Southport,
PR8 2LX
www.royalbirkdale.com
Phone: +44 (0) 1704 552020
Email: secretary@royalbirkdale.com

General course information –

Par: 72 (White) / 72 (Yellow) / 75 (Red)

S.S.S: 74 (White) / 72 (Yellow) / 75 (Red)

Slope rating: 138 (White) / 132 (Yellow) / 138 (Red)

Length: 5,820yds–6,829yds

Longest hole: Par-5 15th, 543yds (White) / Par-5 17th, 449yds–508yds (Red/Yellow)

Shortest hole: Par-3 7th, 111yds–178yds

Type: Links

Handicap Certificate: Required (maximum handicap is 28 for men and 36 for ladies).

Green fees:
(Low season)
● per round* (Weekday)
* = includes soup and a sandwich before/after your round.

(High season)
● per round (Weekday & Weekend)

Caddies: £50.00 per player per round (+ gratuity) paid in cash directly to the caddie. Must be booked in advance via Managing Secretary's office.

Equipment hire:
Limited number of buggies available if required on medical grounds. Clubs and pull trolleys can be hired from the pro shop, +44 (0) 1704 552030.

How do I book a round of golf?

Royal Birkdale welcomes visitors at the following times during the week to play the championship links course:

Monday/ Wednesday/ Thursday	All day (after 9.30 am)
Tuesday	Afternoons from 2.10 pm
Friday	Limited availability
Sundays	Afternoons during high season only

There are three ways to book a round of golf at Royal Birkdale Golf Club:

Online:
www.royalbirkdale.com/Visitor Booking

Price Guide: ● up to £49 | ● £50 – £99 | ● £100 – £149 | ● £150 – £200 | ● over £200

Phone:
Via the Managing Secretary's office,
+44 (0) 1704 552020

Email:
secretary@royalbirkdale.com

The Birkdale Experience: £295.00
(2020 price). Includes a round of golf,
memorabilia tour, 2-course lunch or dinner and a gift bag. For further
details and to make a reservation
contact the Managing Secretary's
office (via email or telephone).

HISTORY

In the summer of 1961, Arnold Palmer arrived in Southport for the 90th
edition of The Open Championship, still smarting after coming so close to
lifting the claret jug at his first attempt, missing out by one stroke to Ken
Nagle, the year before.

Despite gale-force winds and heavy rain, Palmer was determined to get
his hands on golf's ultimate prize. Leading by four strokes on the final round,
disaster struck on the 15th hole (now the 16th) when a wayward tee-shot saw
his ball land beneath a blackberry bush.

'The King' only knew one way to play – attack! Rather than play out
sideways, accepting a likely dropped shot in the process, he reached for his
6-iron and swung as hard as he could catching enough of the ball to land it
on the green. He would go on to win The Open by just one stroke.

There is now a commemorative plaque at the spot on the course where
Palmer nailed his approach, confirming his reputation as a golfing superstar
(a year later he would defend his crown at Royal Troon) and that of Royal
Birkdale as a venue where special players become Champion Golfer of the
Year.

The Birkdale Golf Club was formed on 30 July 1889 following a meeting
held at the home of one of nine founding members. By October the original
9-hole course, located at Shaw Hills, was ready for play. After eight years, the
decision was made to relocate to an 18-hole layout at Birkdale Hills where
the club has remained ever since.

Originally designed by local Lytham professional, George Lowe, the course
underwent a major redesign in 1935 by Fred Hawtree and J.H. Taylor, which
included construction of the art deco clubhouse so instantly recognisable
and synonymous with the club today. King George VI bestowed the Royal
Charter upon the club in November 1951.

The fabulous clubhouse at Royal Birkdale shines brightly in front of the 18th green.
Royal Birkdale Golf Club

The list of events hosted by Royal Birkdale throughout its illustrious history reads as a roll call of golf's most prestigious tournaments. No other club in the world has hosted more championships and international competitions since the end of the Second World War.

Naturally, this list includes twice playing host to The Ryder Cup (1965 & 1969). The '69 match resulted in the first ever tied contest and is enshrined in Ryder Cup folklore due to 'the concession'.

At the finale to what had been quite a fractious contest between both teams, Jack Nicklaus produced a truly incredible act of sportsmanship by conceding Tony Jacklin's 3ft putt. Many observers at the time thought Jacklin still had a bit left to do.

Would Jacklin have missed? As Nicklaus said at the time (much to the dismay of his captain, Sam Snead), he didn't think it was fair to give him the chance.

PLAYING THE COURSE

History tells us that when The Open comes to Royal Birkdale, as it has on ten occasions during the tournament's history, only a player who is at the very top of their game will become Champion Golfer of the Year. There have been no 'left field' victories here.

Of the previous winners, five have been back-to-back champions (Thomson / Palmer/ Trevino/ Watson/ Harrington) and three have won other majors during the same year (Trevino – US Open / O'Meara – The Masters / Harrington – PGA). The subtle message here is simple: if you bring your best, you'll reap the rewards.

With this in mind, the championship course at Royal Birkdale is everything you hope it will be – a tough but fair challenge where every shot matters. Any well-struck tee-shot that finds the fairway will stay on the fairway. Any poorly struck shot will find trouble. No peculiar bounces, humps or hollows to throw your ball off track. Play the course as you see it.

In order to truly cherish the moments you spend walking in the footsteps of Palmer, Trevino, Miller and Spieth as they marched towards the claret jug, it's worth remembering that you will enjoy yourself a lot more if you think your way round, rather than try and blast your way round.

Be smart, not cavalier, and you will give yourself a day to remember.

Most courses ease you in with a nice, gentle opening hole. Royal Birkdale isn't one of them, so make sure you've done all your stretches and taken more than a few practice swings before you face, quite possibly, one of the toughest opening holes, not just on The Open rota, but anywhere in the British Isles.

Your opening tee-shot needs to find the fairway to give yourself a chance of making a positive score. Your approach shot, towards a large, relatively flat green, needs to clear three bunkers at the front, both right and left.

After two more testing par-4s, hole 4 is the first, and longest, of four par-3s. Playing from an elevated tee towards a green 30ft below with three, well positioned, deep bunkers front-left and one front-right. If you're still on your handicap-par by this point, allow yourself a little pat on the back.

The 6th is the first par-5 from the front tees, par-4 from the Championship tees, and is a sweeping dogleg-right towards an uphill, sloping green surrounded by sand dunes and two bunkers protecting the front. Before you reach the putting surface your drive needs to navigate past bunkers on either side of the fairway.

No bunkers at the 10th green but plenty of other natural hazards await any stray approach shots.
Royal Birkdale Golf Club

After a short par-3 and two more tricky par-4s, you reach the turn and the 10th, another par-4, shaping round to the left. Your drive needs to split the fairway between two bunkers either side waiting to catch your ball. This is one of the few holes on the course where longer hitters can attempt to be bold with their drivers.

(12) SIGNATURE HOLE: PAR-3 12TH, 130YDS–183YDS.
Not the longest of the par-3s on the course, but without doubt, one of the most pleasing on the eye. This is a difficult tee-shot towards a kidney-shaped green, protected by a large bunker front-left and one front-right. As an extra shield the green is also surrounded by mounds of thick rough adding extra complication to any up and down attempt.

Pot bunkers guard the front of the 12th green at Royal Birkdale. *Royal Birkdale Golf Club*

If you're playing from the back tees you may have noticed something missing so far – a par-5. You have to wait until the 15th before one arrives. When you finally reach what is the start of any four-hole playoff to decide who wins The Open, you'll find a hole with thirteen bunkers flanking both sides of the fairway and a further two guarding the front of a green that slopes towards them.

Big hitters may fancy their chances at the 15th of picking up a shot, but beware – any putt from the back will be quick, so steady hands are needed to avoid spoiling your chances right at the end.

The 16th and 17th holes are where Royal Birkdale has secured its place in Open folklore. Arnold Palmer's 6-iron approach to the 16th green from underneath a blackberry bush in 1961 (see if you can find the plaque on the fairway) and Padraig Harrington's monster 270yd second shot from the 17th fairway to set up an eagle in 2008 will forever be etched into our memories.

The 16th fairway leading up to the green. The turning point for Arnold Palmer's triumph in the 1961 Open Championship. *Royal Birkdale Golf Club*

Finally, the 18th brings you back towards Royal Birkdale's iconic clubhouse. As was true with the 1st hole, your round ends with a real test. Anything too far right off the tee could be out of bounds and your approach needs to steer clear of three bunkers guarding the front of the green.

HILLSIDE GOLF CLUB
Hastings Road,
Hillside,
Southport,
PR8 2LU
www.hillside-golfclub.co.uk
Phone: +44 (0) 1704 567169
Email: secretary@hillside-golfclub.co.uk

General course information –

Par: 72 (Black/White/Blue/Yellow) / 75 (Red)

S.S.S: 75 (Black) / 74 (White) / 73 (Blue) / 71 (Yellow) / 75 (Red)

Slope rating: 138 (Black) / 137 (White) / 136 (Blue) / 128 (Yellow) / 140 (Red)

Length: 5,888yds–7,078yds

Longest hole: Par-5 17th, 488yds–547yds

Shortest hole: Par-3 7th, 141yds–170yds

Type: Links

Handicap Certificate: Required

Green fees:
(Low season)
● per round (weekdays)
● per round (Sunday)

(Shoulder season)
● per round (weekdays / Sunday)

(High season)
● per round (weekdays)
● per round (Saturday & Sunday)

Caddies: Available. Book in advance via the office, +44 (0) 1704 567169

Equipment hire:
Clubs, buggies and trolleys can be hired from the pro shop (+44 (0) 1704 568360)

How do I book a round of golf?
Hillside welcomes visitors at the following times during the week:

Monday/ Thursday/ Friday	9.04 am–12.00 noon / from 2.00 pm
Tuesday (Ladies Day)	from 2.00 pm
Wednesday	1.36 pm–3.36 pm
Saturday	Limited availability (after 3.30 pm)
Sunday	12.00 noon–2.00 pm

There are two ways to book a round of golf at Hillside Golf Club:

Phone:
+44 (0) 1704 567169

Email:
secretary@hillside-golfclub.co.uk

Price Guide: ● up to £49 | ● £50 – £99 | ● £100 – £149 | ● £150 – £200 | ● over £200

HISTORY

Hillside Golf Club was officially formed following a meeting at the Portland Hotel in the summer of 1911. Very little is known about the first twelve years of its existence, other than the founding members played their golf on a 9-hole course left behind by Blundell Golf Club who had moved to another site in Ainsdale that same year (eventually disbanding in 1935).

This original course was situated on the other side of the railway tracks to Hillside's current location; however, by 1922 another site was required to cater

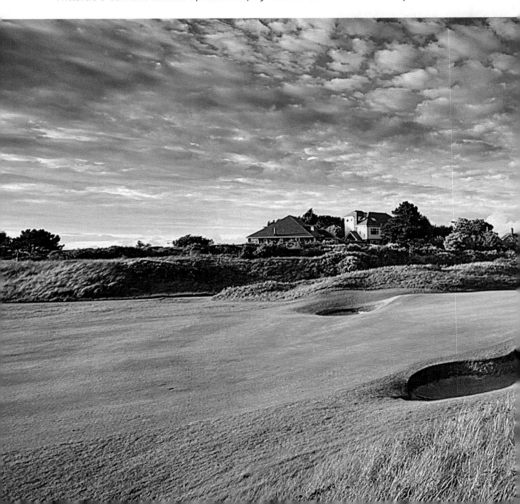

for the ever-growing membership. A decision was made to move across the tracks to a patch of land available to lease from the Weld Blundell Estate.

The new course layout was ready for play on 4 August 1923 – constructed and designed by Conway of Halifax, with the clubhouse opening the following year on 19 December 1924, parts of which still form the current structure.

By 1957, the club was ready to consider changes to its layout, appointing acclaimed architect, Fred Hawtree, with the task of reconstructing large

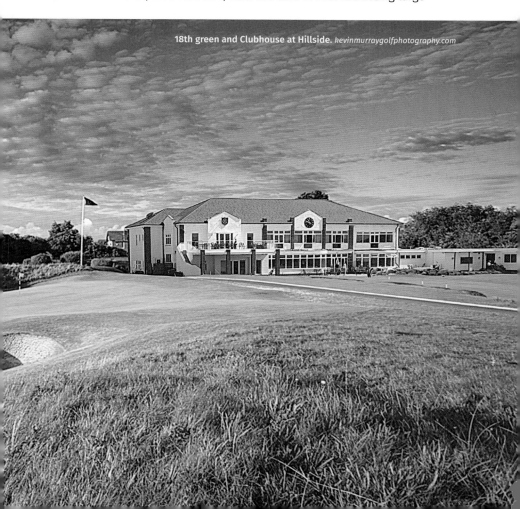

18th green and Clubhouse at Hillside. *kevinmurraygolfphotography.com*

sections of the course. This involved the exchange of land containing four holes at the far end of the course with an area of unused land between Hillside and Royal Birkdale. The new championship course was ready for play in 1967.

Hillside has played host to both the Amateur Championships and Ladies Amateur Championships and has been a Final Qualifying course for The Open over a dozen times.

In 2019 Hillside was selected by the European Tour as host venue for the British Masters in association with local professional, Tommy Fleetwood. Marcus Kinhult would emerge victorious, winning by one stroke. This was the first European Tour event to be held at Hillside since the PGA Championships in 1982, when Tony Jacklin beat Bernhard Langer in a play-off.

In 2018 the club commissioned renowned architect Martin Ebert of Mackenzie & Ebert to assess the whole course and develop a framework for future development. Phase 1 commenced in winter 2019, with work being carried out on the 1st, 9th and 18th holes, as well as improvements to the Practice Facilities.

PLAYING THE COURSE

An oft-repeated parable about Hillside refers to an unsolicited letter the club received from Greg Norman following the 1982 PGA Championship, in which he describes the back-9 holes as the best in Britain.

While there is ample evidence to support Norman's assessment – the homeward loop at Hillside is undoubtedly a unique golfing experience with each hole perfectly framed among monumental sand dunes within the most glorious, tranquil surroundings – the 'tale of two halves' narrative tends to slightly undervalue what is also a thoroughly enjoyable outward section.

The links course at Hillside combines two distinctive loops of nine to provide a solid, strategic test of golf from the opening hole to the last.

The 1st hole is almost a mirror image of the famous starting hole at Prestwick. This time, the railway line, that most treasured feature of a links course, runs all the way along the left-hand side of the hole rather than the right. Anyone with a vicious slice doesn't get away that easily, as three pot bunkers line the right of the fairway. Only straight and true will do for your opening swing.

After the opening hole, most of the longer holes on the front-9 provide a series of risk/reward opportunities, tempting you into getting as close as you can to a variety of hazards in order to leave the best angle into the greens.

The green surrounded by trees and bunkers at Hillside's par-3 7th hole. *kevinmurraygolfphotography.com*

Hole 2 is the first par-5 and a definite three-shot to the green for most. As with the 1st, you have the railway tracks for company along the left-hand side of the fairway. Aiming left with your drive and second shot provides the best line into a green sloping back to front. You should avoid being too ambitious with your approach towards the green at the tricky par-4 3rd, as anything pushed too far right may find the pond on this side of the fairway.

The 7th is a fairly straightforward par-3, albeit beautifully framed, surrounded by pine trees and sand dunes along the left and behind the green. Holes 8 and 9 are both par-4s with fairly open, generous fairways. Best to avoid trying to drive over the road at the 9th unless you can comfortably carry 300yds from the tee.

The drama of the inward-9 starts with a par-3 at the 10th. Typically played into the prevailing wind, if you find the putting surface with your tee shot allow yourself a hearty pat on the back. Anything short could find bunkers both left and right at the front of the green.

11 **SIGNATURE HOLE: PAR-5 11TH, 481YDS–509YDS.**
Indulge yourself for a few moments once you reach the tee box here to take in the astonishing, panoramic views above the sand dunes, out towards the coast and also capturing parts of both neighbouring courses either side of Hillside.

Nothing less than your driver will do, down towards the fairway, flanked by sand dunes as it curves to the left and rises towards a green with pine trees surrounding the back. A par at this hole is one to treasure.

View from the tee-box high above the fairway at the par-5 11th. *Hillside Golf Club*

The 12th is a classic two-shot par-4 with a water hazard waiting for any drive pushed too far to the right. The tee box at the 14th provides more stunning views out towards Blackpool in the north and Snowdonia in the south.

Hole 16 is the last par-3 and has no bunkers – it doesn't need them. This is one of the toughest par-3s in England. It's long (218yds from the back tees) but often plays downwind toward a two-tiered green. Whatever club you choose just give it all you've got.

The 17th is another majestic par-5 to rival the 11th. Out of bounds lingers all along the left side of the fairway. Anything pushed too far in this direction may reach the 18th hole at Royal Birkdale, so, best to keep right.

Your drive on the 18th needs to aim as close as you can to the trio of bunkers on the right of the fairway for the best line toward a putting surface patrolled by two deep bunkers at the front. Make your last approach your best and aim straight for the centre of the green.

Fairway leading towards the 15th green with the Irish Sea in the distance. *Hillside Golf Club*

SOUTHPORT & AINSDALE GOLF CLUB

Bradshaws Lane,
Ainsdale,
Southport,
Merseyside,
PR8 3LG
www.sandagolfclub.co.uk
Phone: +44 (0) 1704 578000
Email: admin@sandagolf.co.uk

General course information –
Par: 72 (White) / 71 (Yellow) / 74 (Red)
S.S.S: 74 (White) / 72 (Yellow) / 75 (Red)
Slope rating: 138 (White) / 130 (Yellow) / 137 (Red)
Length: 5,665yds–6,803yds
Longest hole: Par-5 2nd, 472yds–566yds
Shortest hole: Par-3 8th, 128yds–153yds
Type: Links

(Yellow and red tees available for visitors)

Handicap Certificate: Not required

Green fees:
(Low season)
● per round (Weekends & Bank Holidays)
● per round (Monday-Friday)

(Shoulder season)
● per round

(High season)
● per round

Caddies:
£55 per player per round (+ gratuity). Must be booked in advance via pro shop (+44 1704 577316)

Equipment hire:
Buggies, clubs and pull trolleys can be hired from the pro shop

How do I book a round of golf?
Southport & Ainsdale welcomes visitors at any time during the week except Thursday (before 12 noon) and Saturday (before 3.30 pm)

There are two ways to book a round of golf at Southport & Ainsdale Golf Club:

Phone:
+44 (0) 1704 577316 or +44 (0) 1704 578000

Email:
jimpaynegolf@gmail.com or admin@sandagolfclub.co.uk

Price Guide: ● up to £49 | ● £50 – £99 | ● £100 – £149 | ● £150 – £200 | ● over £200

HISTORY

In January 1906, members of a Birkdale whist society began to explore the possibility of a new golf club in the village. By Whit Saturday of the same year, on a glorious sunny afternoon, twenty-seven ladies and twenty-four men gathered on Birkdale common for a mixed competition on a rudimentary 9-hole course (using jam pots for holes) to declare the newly formed Grosvenor Golf Club open.

Before the end of the year, the club would adopt a new name – Southport & Ainsdale. Despite the course residing in Birkdale, the name was agreed in order to placate the nearby Birkdale and Southport (now known as Hesketh) clubs. The new title offered the opportunity to use the abbreviation S&A, a sobriquet associated with the club ever since.

A new 18-hole course, laid out by Lytham's club professional, George Lowe, was open for play by June 1907. The club wasted no time in raising its profile among the golfing elite. An exhibition match in 1917, to raise funds for the war effort, could count on two members of the great triumvirate – James Braid and John Henry Taylor – among the competitors.

The sun sets over the links at Southport & Ainsdale. *Southport & Ainsdale Golf Club*

Revered in equal measure as both a golfer and course architect, Braid would return five years later to leave a more permanent stamp on the course layout. Following a council directive forcing the club to concede land for the construction of a road link, the five-time Champion Golfer of the Year was tasked with redesigning six new holes – the 1st, 2nd, 6th, 7th, 8th and 18th.

S&A would offer its services as host for many professional tournaments during the infancy of the European Tour. Jack Nicklaus took his first overseas bow at S&A in the 1962 Piccadilly Tournament, won by 5-times Open Champion Peter Thomson. Arnold Palmer also played here during the Nine Nations tournament in 1965.

Of all the tournaments held at S&A, it is the Ryder Cup which the club is most proud having had the honour on two occasions – 1933 and 1937.

The match in 1933 was one of the most dramatic in Ryder Cup history. Great Britain triumphed over the USA 6½ – 5½ with the whole match coming down to the last putt on the final green, Denny Shute of the USA missing a 6ft putt that would have retained the trophy for his team (less than two weeks later, Shute would become Champion Golfer of the Year at St Andrews).

Four years later the two teams would meet again, but this time the Americans would triumph convincingly by a score of 8 – 4. This was the first occasion a host nation lost on home soil in the Ryder Cup. The USA, having regained the trophy two years prior, would not taste defeat again until 1957.

PLAYING THE COURSE

The links course at Southport & Ainsdale is a wily old fox with an unconventional layout that instinctively knows how to keep you interested from beginning to end. Regardless of ability or handicap, this is a course that gives every golfer a chance, tempting you to take risks without gifting you a clear view of the reward.

There is no traditional 'nine out, nine back' route here. Instead you follow two sets of loops with holes 2 to 6 forming an inner loop, and the remaining holes an outer loop.

Sitting slightly inland from the coast, despite the absence of a sea view, this is a classic links course in an exquisite setting where the stillness is only disturbed by the pleasantly familiar sound of trains trundling down the neighbouring railway track.

If you're hoping for a gentle start to your round, you've no such luck, beginning with a dreaded par-3, swiftly followed by the longest hole on

No less than nine bunkers surround the green at the 1st hole. *Southport & Ainsdale Golf Club*

the course. With this in mind, make sure you give yourself time to warm up before you head to the starter's hut.

At 185yds from the yellow tees, the 1st hole will definitely shake off any cobwebs. In addition to the length, there's also the small matter of hitting towards a small green surrounded by nine bunkers. Depending on the wind, anything from a mid-iron to a driver could be required. Your first swing at S&A, with the clubhouse crowd looking on, needs to be right on the money.

From the tee box at the par-5 2nd, you can see all the way down the fairway to the green. Seeing where you need to go doesn't make this hole any easier as the narrow fairway (a constant feature at S&A) is flanked with bunkers on either side. Three accurate shots will see you safely on the green and a chance for your par.

The remaining four holes of the inner loop are all par-4s of varying difficulty. The 5th is the toughest hole on the course – a long, straight fairway that demands an equally straight drive, followed by an imposing approach shot toward an awkward, semi-blind green.

At 490yds from the white tees, the par-5 7th gives longer hitters a chance to reach the green in two as you start your way round the outer loop section. The short par-3 8th is a rarity with no bunkers, particularly at a course littered

A narrow fairway greets you at the 2nd tee. *Southport & Ainsdale Golf Club*

with them. However, the elevated green ensures any par-score here will be hard-fought – just don't be short!

As with the front-9, the back-9 also starts with a difficult, mid-distance par-3. Anything short or right will fall off the green, anything on target should find the centre.

The 15th is a fairly short par-4 and the calm before the closing storm ahead. Keep to the right side of the fairway for the best line into the green.

16 **SIGNATURE HOLE: PAR-5 16TH, 455YDS–528YDS, 'GUMBLEYS'.**
Site of the legendary Gumbleys bunker. Named after one of S&A's original members, Hobart Gumbley, who fought to keep the huge sandhill that splits the fairway intact, when others favoured reducing its height so players had a clear sight of the green.

Your tee-shot eases you into the hole before you take on your second shot, which must clear this mammoth mound of sand, completely blinded from the fairway beyond. Aim over the centre and you should be fine.

Anything below your handicap-par here is something to savour.

The 16th green, beyond Gumbleys bunker. If you're here in two shots allow yourself a wry smile.
Southport & Ainsdale Golf Club

After the epic 16th take a breather and admire the fabulous vista from the 17th tee box all the way toward the clubhouse. Once you've caught your breath you have a formidable par-4 to navigate, facing the wind, with the railway line running along the right of the fairway. Your approach should aim long as all the trouble is at the front of the green.

If you reach the 18th still ahead on your handicap score after the last two holes, allow yourself a smile. Keep it sensible here and aim for the widest part of the fairway for a chance to hit the centre of the green with your approach, avoiding trouble both at the front and off the back.

FORMBY GOLF CLUB
Golf Road,
Freshfield,
Liverpool,
L37 1LQ
www.formbygolfclub.co.uk
Phone: +44 (0) 1704 872164
Email: teetimes@formbygolfclub.co.uk

General course information –
Par: 72 (All tees)
S.S.S: 76 (Blue) / 75 (White) / 73 (Yellow) / 71 – Men / 77 – Ladies (Red)
Slope rating: 144 (Blue) / 141 (White) / 142 (Yellow) / 136 – Men / 149 – Ladies (Red)
Length: 6,060yds–7075yds
Longest hole: Par-5 3rd, 486yds–561yds
Shortest hole: Par-3 16th, 115yds–140yds
Type: Links

Handicap Certificate: Required (maximum handicap is 28 for men and 36 for ladies)

Green fees:
(Low season)
● per round (Monday–Friday)
● per round (Sunday)

(Shoulder season)
● per round (Monday-Friday)
● per round (Weekend)

(High season)
● per day (Monday-Friday)
● per day (Weekend)

Caddies:
£50.00 per player per round (+ gratuity) paid in cash directly to the caddie. Must be booked in advance via +44 (0) 1704 872164.

Equipment hire:
Two buggies are available upon advanced request. Clubs and pull trolleys can be hired from the pro shop +44 (0) 1704 873090.

How do I book a round of golf?
Formby welcomes visitors at any time Monday-Friday. During the summer months, tee-times on Saturday are available after 3.30 pm and after 2.30 pm on Sundays.

During the winter months tee-times are also available on Sundays between 10am-11am.

There are three ways to book a round of golf at Formby Golf Club:

Online:
www.formbygolfclub.co.uk/The Experience/Green Fees

Phone:
+44 (0) 1704 872164

Email:
teetimes@formbygolfclub.co.uk OR info@formbygolfclub.co.uk

Price Guide: ● up to £49 | ● £50 – £99 | ● £100 – £149 | ● £150 – £200 | ● over £200

Formby clubhouse stands proudly in front of the 18th green. *kevinmurraygolfphotography.com*

HISTORY

In 1909 Formby Golf Club was the recipient of two gifts, both of which have long since become iconic images entwined within the fabric of its distinguished history. When you think of Formby, you think of the clock tower and the hippopotamus.

Mr Bruce Ismay, Chairman of the White Star Line, presented the clock to the club, which sits atop the tower on the southwest corner of the clubhouse. Three years later, Mr Ismay rather fortuitously survived the sinking of his company's most famous ship, the Titanic.

The Hippo's head, which resides next to a stairway separating the main clubhouse lounge, was given to the club by the widow of a founding member who captured the animal during a hunting trip to Africa and has a more compelling story to tell.

During World War II, Formby's clubhouse was used as an officer's mess. After one particularly heavy 'session' before embarking on a mission, a group of sailors decided to commandeer the hippo and take it with them on their ship. So, off the hippo went, strapped to a searchlight platform, to fight the 'Battle of Narvik' in the Norwegian fjords. Eventually, it was returned to the club along with a heartfelt apology from all of those involved in the 'hippo hijack'.

Every year, members commemorate the incident when they compete in the Hippo Competition.

Along with many other golf clubs across the UK, Formby – founded in December 1884 – has the railway to thank for its formation as the network threaded its way around the northwest at the height of the Victorian era. The course (originally a 9-hole layout, extended to 18 holes around the turn of the century) resides within easy walking distance of Freshfield Station.

In 1896, Formby Ladies Golf Club was established. A new clubhouse facility was built for the members alongside their own 18-hole course within the grounds of the Formby Golf Club estate.

Some of golf's most prominent architects from the last century have left their hallmark on the links at Formby, among them, James Braid, Willie Park Jr and Harry Colt. In 1980 Donald Steel oversaw wide-ranging alterations to the course due to extensive coastal erosion, rebuilding holes 7, 8 and 9.

Formby has a proud association with amateur golf and has played host to some of the most prestigious tournaments – the Brabazon, the Amateur championship and the Curtis Cup in 2004. At 14 years old, Michelle Wie became the youngest player in Curtis Cup history when she competed for the USA at Formby, winning her singles matches handsomely to claim two points towards her team's victory.

The 2009 Amateur Championship, held during the club's 125th anniversary year, saw 16-year-old Matteo Manassero become the youngest ever winner of the tournament.

In 1984, during the club's centenary year, two future Ryder Cup captains battled it out for the Amateur championship with Jose Maria Olazabal emerging triumphant over Colin Montgomerie.

PLAYING THE COURSE

Nestled right in the heart of England's golf coast, with its more famous Royal neighbours north and south, Formby's elegant championship course is a links experience with a difference.

In addition to all the traditional elements you would expect from a links layout – undulating greens, fast fairways and deep bunkers – this charming, natural, hybrid design also offers a heathland ambience with pine trees enclosing the course on three sides.

The constant sea breeze provides you with a timely reminder, regardless of the surroundings, it is a links challenge that lies ahead. If you're to avoid the punishing sand traps or chipping out from among the trees, driving accuracy will need to be at a premium.

Rather than adopting a one-dimensional layout, the course follows a more unconventional, looping route where the angle of each hole toward the ocean determines the wind direction you're up against. This is a truly alluring location for golf, but one that's not afraid to play ugly.

The first three holes at Formby run alongside the railway track behind the tree line so best to avoid straying too far right from the tee. The par-5 3rd is the longest hole on the course. Big hitters can make the green in two shots but it may be more sensible to lay up before the mid-fairway bunker leaving you a pitch into a tricky two-tiered green.

The 4th is a terrific short par-4 where all your senses will tell you to get the driver out but more conventional wisdom dictates there really is no point as the bunker placement here is lethal. Best to layup and rely on your approach to navigate on to the green.

Holes 6 & 7 (both par-4s) illustrate the real beauty of the links/heathland crossover at Formby. The 6th plays as a links hole – tight fairway to an elevated green surrounded by dunes. The 7th has a real heathland feel, flanked by trees on either side of the fairway towards a green sloping back to front. Two par scores here should be cherished.

At the end of a glorious day on the North West coast, the sun goes down over the 8th green at Formby. *Formby Golf Club*

The sea is just visible beyond the trees sheltering the 9th green at Formby.
kevinmurraygolfphotography.com

Holes 8 & 9 both provide the welcome distraction of your first glimpse of the sea. The views on this part of the course are astonishingly beautiful and a highlight of many who have played here. Use them as motivation to navigate through two of the toughest holes on the course.

The scenic elevated tee at the par-4 9th may leave you with bated breath, but you still need to compose yourself and hit a straight drive, bisecting two fairway bunkers ready to catch your ball. Your approach should aim left to catch the best line into the green. If you drop shots on this hole take solace in the fact the view will stay with you long after you've forgotten any blots on your scorecard.

Holes 11 to 15, all testing par-4s, are a stretch of terrific links holes and arguably the most challenging section of the course. All the trouble is down the right-hand side from the tee at the 11th. The fairway sits below the putting surface leaving a partially sighted approach towards a plateau green surrounded by large dunes.

(12) SIGNATURE HOLE: PAR-4 12TH, 320YDS–421YDS.
As with the previous hole, your tee-shot needs to stay left to keep clear of all the trouble along the right of the fairway and give yourself the best approach in to a raised green, protected by a large, cavernous bunker front-left. Best to aim towards the back of the green for the best chance of what would be a prized-par score.

The 16th is the shortest hole on the course with all the trouble at the front so aim towards the back of the green for the best chance of a positive result. After the final par-5 at the 17th, the clubhouse comes back into view. The 18th is a demanding closing hole with an approach shot towards a long narrow green surrounded by four bunkers.

18-hole courses nearby

● FORMBY LADIES GOLF CLUB

Not so much nearby as, literally, bang in the middle. Formed in 1896, Formby Ladies Golf club resides within the perimeter of Formby Golf Club's championship course.

Visitors (both male and female) are always assured a warm welcome, with tee-times available all week. A demanding layout providing a marvellous, varied, test across all handicap levels.

Website: www.formbyladiesgolfclub.co.uk
Email: secretary@formbyladiesgolfclub.co.uk
Telephone: +44 (0) 1704 873493

Par: 71
Length: 5,374yds
Type: Links

Fees:
● per round (Weekday & Weekend)

10

THE WEST LANCASHIRE GOLF CLUB

Hall Road West,
Blundellsands,
Liverpool,
L23 8SZ
www.westlancashiregolf.co.uk
Phone: +44 (0) 151 924 1076
Email: golf@westlancashiregolf.co.uk

General course information – Men:

Par: 72 (Black/White) / 71 (Yellow) / 70 (Blue)

S.S.S: 75 (Black) / 74 (White) / 71 (Yellow) / 67 (Blue)

Slope rating: 140 (Black) / 138 (White) / 135 (Yellow) / 125 (Blue)

Ladies:

Par: 72 (Blue) / 74 (Red)

S.S.S: 74 (Blue) / 76 (Red)

Slope rating: 133 (Blue) / 140 (Red)

Length: 5,460yds–7,016yds

Longest hole: Par-5 11th, 'Railway', 585yds–443yds

Shortest hole: Par-3 6th, 'Hillside', 153yds–101yds (Black Course: Par-3, 3rd, 'Bowl', 154yds)

Type: Links

Handicap Certificate: Not required (A wide variety of tees and course layouts exist to ensure golfers of all abilities are welcome. If unsure which tees to use, check with the pro shop upon arrival.)

Green fees:
(Low season)
● per round (weekdays)

(Shoulder season)
● per round (weekdays)
● per round (weekend)

(High season)
● per round (weekdays & weekends)

Caddies:
£50.00 per round. Caddie fees to be paid in cash + gratuity. (Advanced booking recommended via professional@westlancashiregolf.co.uk / +44 (0) 151 924 1076 – option 2)

Equipment hire:
Clubs, buggies (six available – recommended to book in advance if required) electric trolleys and pull trolleys can be hired from the pro shop.

How do I book a round of golf?
The West Lancashire welcomes visitors at all times during the week.

Price Guide: ● up to £49 | ● £50 – £99 | ● £100 – £149 | ● £150 – £200 | ● over £200

There are three ways to book a round of golf at The West Lancashire Golf Club:

Online:
www.westlancashiregolf.co.uk/
Visitors/Green fees

Phone:
+44 (0) 151 924 1076

Email:
golf@westlancashiregolf.co.uk

HISTORY

Founded in 1873 by a group of seven existing members of Royal Liverpool Golf Club, West Lancashire has the distinction of being the oldest golf club in the county (albeit Blundellsands now officially resides in Merseyside following the county's creation in 1974) and one of the oldest golf clubs in England.

The West Lancashire Ladies Golf Club followed in 1891 and was the first ladies club formed in Lancashire.

Originally, membership of both Hoylake and West Lancashire was shared, and by 1903 five club captains of West Lancashire also had the same honour at Royal Liverpool.

West Lancashire Golf Club has always been a keen advocate of The Amateur Championship and was one of twenty-four clubs that subscribed to the cost of the trophy in 1885.

One of the most famous 'shared' members was two-time Open Champion, Harold Hilton (joining in 1889), becoming West Lancashire's first paid secretary in 1901 – the same year he won the second of his four Amateur Championships.

Previous Open Champions who also spent time as club professionals at West Lancashire include Sandy Herd (1902) and Arthur Havers (1923).

Part of West Lancashire's mystique is that the architect of the original course, initially a rudimentary 9-hole layout, is unknown. Some of golf's finest designers would lend their hand to later alterations and expansion to 18 holes covering land on either side of the railway line, most notably, James Braid.

In order to bring the entire course across onto the seaward side of the railway line, acclaimed designer, Ken Cotton, was recruited to construct a new layout, which was opened for play in 1961. Continuing with its modernisation drive, a new clubhouse followed a year later.

Fabulous aerial view of the entire links course at West Lancashire. *The West Lancashire Golf Club*

In 1976, four future Masters champions took part in final qualifying at West Lancashire for The Open Championship – Sandy Lyle, Ian Woosnam, Nick Faldo and Bernhard Langer. Both Lyle and Woosnam were still amateurs at the time and failed to make the cut, with only Faldo and Langer progressing to Royal Birkdale.

Since 2005, the adjacent coastline has been further enriched by the addition of Anthony Gormley's 'Another Place'. This installation consists of 100 iron figures cast from the artist's own body shown at different stages rising out of the sand, spread across a 3km stretch of beach and 1km out to sea. The 2nd tee box on the course offers a perfect view of this unique piece of art.

PLAYING THE COURSE

The West Lancashire Golf Club resides in the heart of England's glorious Golf Coast, quietly keeping its own counsel for nearly 150 years away from the glare of publicity that surrounds its distinguished royal neighbours.

While the attraction of playing on an Open rota course is understandable, 'West Lancs' offers a more rustic atmosphere. Firm, fast running fairways, flanked by the coastline on one side and a railway line on the other. It's difficult to think of anywhere more 'links' than this. When you visit here, be prepared to become a fan for life.

The layout is set up as two symmetrical 9-hole loops, starting and finishing at the Clubhouse. When you stand on the tee each hole is clearly laid out in front of you; there are no tricks here. While the rough at West Lancs is not as penal as it once was, if you're to score well you simply have to find the fairways.

Links courses often present a dilemma for big hitters and West Lancs is no exception. All your instincts will tell you to reach for the driver while your gut screams for a long iron. Many of the members will tell you, if in doubt, always go with your gut.

Almost all the greens at West Lancs are raised and shaped like an upturned saucer, making any approach play much more imposing. Anything missing the heart of the green runs the risk of running off the putting surface to leave a testing recovery shot.

The par-4 1st is a pretty formidable opening hole, particularly as it usually plays into the prevailing wind. All the trouble here is along the right side of the fairway so keep left with your tee-shot. A par here is a great start.

On a clear day, from the 2nd tee-box, you can see all the way across the Mersey estuary toward Snowdonia. When the tide is out you can also make out some of the iron figures, which form part of Anthony Gormley's 'Another Place' art installation.

Hole 2 is a short par-5 with the chance to reach the green in two. The bunkers, as with the rest of the course, are perilously positioned to catch your ball off the tee and the same with your approach where three bunkers surround the front of the green leaving just a narrow gap to navigate through.

The views from the par-4 4th tee are jaw-dropping, but be mindful – out of bounds lurks along the left. An accurate tee shot is needed here before your approach towards a green with another narrow entrance and two pot bunkers sitting front-right. A par at this hole should be cherished as much as the vista it provides.

The par-4 7th is a sharp dogleg to the right tempting you to cut off the corner. The penalties for falling short could be pretty severe. If you're not sure best to hit the ball where you can see it and go from there.

Par-3 12th green with the Mersey Estuary's busy shipping lane in the background.
The West Lancashire Golf Club

The par-4 8th offers more stunning sea views from the tee. Be mindful here to take one more club than you think for your approach to reach a large green – nearly 40yds long – with a set of bunkers lurking at the front.

On the back-9, the longest hole on the course – the par-5 11th – is named after that classic links feature, 'Railway', which runs along the right-hand side of the fairway. Your tee-shot must navigate the first set of bunkers and your second shot should steer right for the best angle in to the green.

Hole 12 is a terrific par-3. Your tee-shot must clear the two bunkers sat precariously at the front-right of the green to stand any chance of a par. Best advice, as with the 8th, is to take an extra club than you think you might need.

14 SIGNATURE HOLE: PAR-4 14TH, 355YDS–434YDS, 'BELL'.
The hardest hole on the course and the only one with a blind tee shot. For the perfect line, aim for the church steeple in the distance, avoiding the fairway bunker (the only one at this hole) lurking on the right of the fairway. Only the longest hitters will be left with an unobstructed view of the green. If you can't see it, play short and left.

The putting surface is protected by woodland along the right and off the back. Some green complexes don't need any surrounding bunkers to make them any more intimidating – this is one of them.

The final hole, another par-4, is a hard green to find in two shots. Your drive needs to land between the fairway bunkers on the left and the large pond on the right. For your last approach, try a classic links shot – low and running – to find the putting surface.

A lone golfer makes their way down the 13th fairway at West Lancs. *The West Lancashire Golf Club*

11

WALLASEY GOLF CLUB

Bayswater Road,
Wallasey,
Wirral,
CH45 8LA
www.wallaseygolfclub.com
Phone: +44 (0) 151 691 1024
Email: office@wallaseygolfclub.com

General course information –
Par: 72 (Yellow) / 74 (Red)

S.S.S: 72 (Yellow) / 75 (Red)

Slope rating: 132 (Yellow) / 140 (Red)

Length: 5,825yds–6,319yds

Longest hole: Par-5 13th, 'Cop',
488yds–528yds

Shortest hole: Par-3 12th, 'Old Glory',
126yds–137yds

Type: Links

Handicap Certificate: Not required*

* = Whilst a recognised handicap is
not required, golfers should be able
to play to a competent standard for
both their own enjoyment and to
maintain a fair pace of play.

Green fees:
(Low season)
● per round (Weekday & Weekend)

(High season)
● per round (Weekday & Weekend)

Caddies:
£50 per round (+ gratuity). Must be
booked in advance.

Equipment hire:
Pull trolleys, electric trolleys and
clubs can be hired from the pro
shop. There are no buggies available,
however, visitors may use their own
(single seat) with prior notice and
approval from the club.

How do I book a round of golf?
Wallasey welcomes visitors at
any time with the exception of
Wednesdays and Saturdays. Tee-
times are available between 9.36 am–
11.52 am and 1.36 pm–3.52 pm.

There are three ways to book a
round of golf at Wallasey Golf Club:

Online:
www.wallaseygolfclub.com/Visitors/
Green fees and Societies

Phone:
Via pro shop, +44 (0) 151 691 1024

Email:
office@wallaseygolfclub.com

Price Guide: ● up to £49 | ● £50 – £99 | ● £100 – £149 | ● £150 – £200 | ● over £200

HISTORY

Wallasey Golf Club was founded in 1891 by a group of members from nearby Royal Liverpool who'd grown tired of their crowded course. The links course has received attention from two legendary golf architects. Old Tom Morris designed the original layout before James Braid orchestrated alterations in 1929 prior to Wallasey's selection as a qualifying course for the 1930 Open Championship.

For all Wallasey's rich history, it is a course that is synonymous with one thing – Stableford, the great golf leveller.

Used all around the world (especially in the UK) by clubs as the ideal scoring system to level the playing field between high and low handicappers, Stableford allows everyone in competitions an equal shot at the trophy. If you were ever intrigued enough to wonder where, and by whom, this system was created, then look no further – it's here.

Dr Frank Stableford, member at Wallasey Golf Club from 1914, observed too many modest club players becoming dispirited after only a few bad holes.

Glorious view from behind the green and back down the fairway at the par-5 4th hole.
James Drake, Specialist Golf Photographer, Northern England

He felt there should be a way for golfers of all abilities to remain interested in their round right up until the last hole. The result was the scoring system named after its creator; used for the first time in a competition at Wallasey on 16 May 1932.

However, it wasn't all plain sailing for the Doctor. He spent many years perfecting the system before presenting his idea to members, whose initial reaction was to suggest their learned golfing practitioner may need to prescribe himself some strong medicine, 'Play golf for points? What rubbish'. Their attitude soon changed following the competition and Stableford was rewarded with the club captaincy in 1933.

Rather ironically (and something many lowly club players will relate to), Dr Stableford never won a competition using the scoring rules that bear his name.

Wallasey also left an indelible impression upon one of the most influential figures in golf's history. Bobby Jones, fresh from his grand slam exploits (including victory at nearby Hoylake in the 1930 Open), was the subject of a portrait painting by Wallasey club member, John A.A. Berrie.

Jones sat for no more than six portraits during his life, but only ever gave his seal of approval – and signature – to the one that sits proudly in Wallasey's main lounge today.

PLAYING THE COURSE

Situated towards the south of England's Golf Coast on the eastern tip of the Wirral Peninsula, the course at Wallasey is everything you could wish for in a true links experience.

Rolling, rugged sand dunes hugging an awe-inspiring coastline, thin fairways toward raised greens, elevated tees and blind shots aplenty. It also has that other key ingredient so synonymous with a links course – the wind! Calm days are extremely rare here so buckle up and be sure to pack warm clothing in your kit bag.

Wallasey may not be the longest course, but many who've played here will tell you that the forces of Mother Nature tend to even things out.

Your round at this intimate and stunningly picturesque course begins with a fairly gentle opening hole before you hit the prevailing wind. Keep right of the two fairway bunkers for the best line into the green, which has a bunker front-right ready to catch any pushed approach shots.

② SIGNATURE HOLE: PAR- 4 2ND, 384YDS–441YDS, 'STABLEFORD'.

The long par-4 2nd is both challenging and historic. This is where Dr Stableford (hence the name) perfected his scoring system, playing the hole countless times, before unleashing it upon the golfing world. Look out for the plaque on the tee box commemorating his achievement.

Try and aim your drive as close to the fairway bunker as you dare. Your approach also needs to be accurate towards a relatively small green. A strong wind makes an already difficult hole much harder. Any 'points' scored here should be cherished.

After a short but nonetheless challenging par-4 at the 3rd (particularly into a strong westerly wind), you reach the point where the course truly reveals itself with incredible views out over the sea at the 4th tee-box, the first par-5 of the round. Steer clear of the boundary fence and you should be okay for your par, unless the wind is really howling.

The fairway loops round toward the green at the famous Stableford hole.
James Drake, Specialist Golf Photographer, Northern England

An accurate drive is needed to hit the narrow fairway at the par-4 3rd hole.
James Drake, Specialist Golf Photographer, Northern England

Hole 5 is the first of four outstanding par-3s at Wallasey. If the wind is up, don't be afraid to get out your driver – you might need it.

The second par-3 at the 9th is named after Bobby Jones and has a plaque in his memory at the tee-box. The original hole played from the 9th tee towards where the 10th green is now and was a particular favourite of his when he played here.

Anything short could be gobbled up by two imposing bunkers at the front, anything long or too far left will leave a tricky chip onto an undulating green where a two-putt is by no means a formality. A three here deserves a pat on the back.

The par-4 11th vies with the 4th for its spectacular setting. The green here is raised and quite undulating making any approach putt very tricky. The long, par-5, 13th is one of the toughest holes on the course, played directly into the wind. The fairway is well protected by bunkers along the left. Anything close to par is a good score.

The difficult home stretch starts at the par-4 15th. Your tee shot needs to stay right of the fairway bunkers and your approach should aim for the back of the green to give you the best chance of two-putting. Hole 17 is the longest par-4 on the course and requires an accurate drive to avoid a blind approach shot into the green.

The 18th is a classic finishing hole towards the clubhouse and village church in the background. Wily old members will tell you to aim for the church tower with your drive. Your approach towards a large green needs to avoid bunkers well positioned to catch anything short and right.

18-hole courses nearby

● LEASOWE GOLF CLUB

Situated right next door to Wallasey Golf Club, this links course shares all the magnificent coastal views with its neighbour.

Website: www.leasowegolfclub.co.uk
Email: office@leasowegolfclub.co.uk
Telephone: +44 (0) 151 677 5852

Par: 71 (Yellow) / 74 (Red)
Length: 5,485yds–6,036yds
Type: Links

Fees:
● per round (Weekdays & Weekends)

● BIDSTON GOLF CLUB

Testing 18-hole parkland course renowned in the area for the condition of its course and the quality of the greens.

Website: www.bidstongolfclub.co.uk
Email: info@bidstongolfclub.co.uk
Telephone: +44 (0) 151 638 3412

Par: 70
Length: 5,268yds–6,153yds
Type: Parkland

Fees:
● per round

12

ROYAL LIVERPOOL GOLF CLUB

Meols Drive,
Hoylake,
Wirral,
CH47 4AL
www.royal-liverpool-golf.com
Phone: +44 (0) 151 632 3101
Email: secretary@royal-liverpool-golf.com

General course information –
Par: 72 (Green & Yellow) / 74 (Red)

S.S.S: 75 (Green & Red) / 73 (Yellow)

Slope rating: 140 (Green) / 135 (Red)

Length: 5,847yds-6,790yds

Longest hole: Par-5 16th, 'Dun', 468yds-552yds

Shortest hole: Par-3 15th, 'Rushes', 100yds-134yds

Type: Links

Handicap Certificate: Required (maximum handicap is 21 for men and 32 for ladies)

Green fees:
(Low season)
● adult per round
● junior per round

(Shoulder season)
● adult per round
● junior per round

(High season)
● adult per round
● junior per round

Caddies:
£50 per golfer per round (+ gratuity). Must be booked in advance via the pro shop, +44 (0) 151 632 5868.

Equipment hire:
Buggies available for visitors with a medical certificate. Pull trolleys, electric trolleys and clubs can be hired from the pro shop.

How do I book a round of golf?
Royal Liverpool welcomes visitors at set times during the week. Visitor tee-times are not usually available at weekends.

There are three ways to book a round of golf at Royal Liverpool Golf Club:

Online:
www.royal-liverpool-golf.com/Visitors/Green Fees/Book a tee time

Phone:
+44 (0) 151 632 7772

Email:
bookings@royal-liverpool-golf.com

Price Guide: ● up to £49 I ● £50 – £99 I ● £100 – £149 I ● £150 – £200 I ● over £200

HISTORY

Throughout The Open's 160-year history only three amateur players have become Champion Golfer of the Year. Of these three, John Ball and Harold Hilton were members of Royal Liverpool Golf Club and the third – Bobby Jones – won his most memorable title in 1930 at Hoylake as part of Golf's first ever Grand Slam.

John Ball was the first ever Englishman to claim the claret jug in 1890. Three months earlier, Ball won The Amateur Championship on his home course, becoming the first man to hold both titles in the same year (Jones is the only other man to replicate this feat). In 2018 Wirral Council unveiled a blue commemorative plaque, placed on one of the club's entrance pillars, in honour of John's golfing achievements.

The Royal Hotel in Hoylake was owned by John's father (John Ball Sr). It was here, following a meeting called by Mr J. Muir Dowie, where The Liverpool Golf Club was officially founded in June 1869. Two years later the club received its royal patronage from Queen Victoria's son, Prince Albert, the Duke of Connaught.

Royal Liverpool holds the distinction of being England's second oldest seaside course after Royal North Devon (founded in 1864). Both these grand old masters have the Morris family to thank for their initial creations. While legendary golf designer, Old Tom Morris, was busy designing the layout around Westward Ho!, his elder brother George (alongside Robert Chambers) was commissioned to construct the course at Hoylake.

View from behind the 10th green looking back down the dogleg fairway.
Kevin Murray and Royal Liverpool Golf Club

For the first seven years of its existence, Royal Liverpool shared its home with the Liverpool Hunt Club, thus the land doubled up as both a golf course and racetrack. After the racing ended, old stables at the rear of the Royal Hotel were converted into a workshop for the club's first professional – Jack Morris (George's son), a position he held for over fifty years.

Royal Liverpool's association with The Open began in 1897 with a victory for local favourite, Harold Hilton (his second title). Despite a thirty-nine year gap between 1967 and 2006, only Royal St George's has hosted the tournament on more occasions in England. In 2023, The Open Championship is scheduled to return to Hoylake for the thirteenth time.

In addition to its connection with professional golf's most famous event, Royal Liverpool is also extremely proud of its pioneering development of the amateur game. Playing host to the first Amateur Championship in 1885 and the inaugural international match between Great Britain & Ireland and the United States in 1921.

Nowadays this prestigious tournament is better known as The Walker Cup, which returned to Hoylake once again in 2019 with Team USA emerging triumphant, 15½ – 10½.

PLAYING THE COURSE

The common-held opinion of the links at Royal Liverpool, upon first sight, is that it seems quite flat with little or no appearance of the undulations and rolling fairways one would expect to see at a course on The Open rota. This is actually quite a deceptive view, which changes as you begin to move through the outward part of the course.

Regardless of any discussions on aesthetics, or whether a true links course must appear so wild upon first sight as to make even the most hardened golfer shake in their plus-fours, this is a layout where Tiger Woods chose to use his driver just the once on the way to his 2006 triumph.

Why? Hoylake was bone dry that week and the most natural links courses are the most unpredictable (and quick). Tiger knew that iron play was the only way to control his ball – and he was right.

Hoylake is as traditional a test of links golf you will find anywhere in the British Isles. Surrounded by properties on three sides and the Dee estuary on the western side, when the wind picks up and howls in from the Irish Sea, the course can really show its teeth.

The round opens with two testing par-4s. The 1st (a par-5 from the Red tees) is a sharp dogleg-right running next to the practice ground that tempts you to aim your drive as close to it as you dare. Your approach also needs to keep left, as out of bounds stretches all the way along the right-hand side up to the bunkerless green.

Keep your drive left at the shorter 2nd, Hoylake's 'Road' hole, to give yourself the best angle in to a green (the only one remaining from the original course layout) protected by three bunkers at the front.

Hole 3 is the first par-5 and requires a threaded drive between gorse on the left and fairway bunkers on the right. The second shot needs to keep right for the best approach toward a difficult, two-tier putting surface.

After the first par-5 comes the first par-3. Newcomers are recommended to take one more club than you feel you need as this hole plays into a crosswind and you may need the extra carry to clear a cavernous bunker lurking at the front-right of the green.

After two testing, lengthy, par-4s and the second par-3 you reach the par-5 8th, known as 'Far' as it's the farthest hole from the clubhouse. If it all goes wrong on this hole, you can console yourself with the knowledge that even the great Bobby Jones scored a seven here on his way to winning the 1930 Open title.

The par-4 9th is where you reach the first of four holes that hug the shoreline providing stunning views out across the estuary.

11 **SIGNATURE HOLE: PAR-3 11TH, 151YDS–194YDS, 'ALPS'.**
The views don't get any better than what you see from the tee-box here. It's hard not to get distracted as you size up what is a tricky tee-shot with the wind in your face towards a sloping green guarded by mounds on the left and a bunker front-right.

Landing left or right won't do any good on this hole. Only straight down the middle will do.

Allow the vista to be your inspiration as you take your swing at the stunning par-3 'Alps'. *Kevin Murray and Royal Liverpool Golf Club*

The 13th hole ('Field') - which, prior to the recent course enhancements played as the 14th - is a long par-5 and the start of a fantastic closing stretch of holes, including the brand new 'Rushes' par-3 - now playing as the 15th. Only big hitters stand a chance of reaching the 13th green in two shots, so best to be smart rather than bold and plot your way to the putting surface.

After one more par-5 at the 16th – the longest hole on the course and plays as the 18th during The Open Championship – hole 17 is named after the Royal Hotel, which acted as the first clubhouse in 1869. Your drive on

The fabulous new par-3 'Rushes' hole only adds to the excitement during an already exhilarating closing stretch at Hoylake. *Sam Cooper and Royal Liverpool Golf Club*

this difficult par-4 needs to stay left for the best line into a long, narrow green regarded as the toughest on the course to putt on. A par at this hole should be treasured.

The par-4 18th requires an accurate drive to avoid fairway bunkers both left and right. Your final approach shot needs to avoid bunkers cleverly positioned around the undulating green, ready to catch any wayward shots.

COURSE ENHANCEMENTS

Royal Liverpool Golf Club recently completed a series of enhancements to its historic links course. The alterations included changes to both the 2nd (raised to produce a flatter landing area, overall size now reduced) and 5th (moved to the left to allow for new 6th hole tee complex) greens.

The most significant change is the creation of a new par-3 'Rushes' hole (100yds-134yds). Players now hit their tee-shot towards an elevated green, looking out toward the Dee estuary. Previously playing as the 13th, 'Rushes' now plays as the member's 15th and the penultimate hole during The Open Championship*.

* = Holes 17 and 18 play as the 1st and 2nd (with the 1st playing as the 3rd and so on) when The Open is played at Royal Liverpool.

18-hole courses nearby

● CALDY GOLF CLUB

Stunning location on the Wirral peninsula with views across the river Dee towards Hilbre Islands and the Welsh mountains beyond. The course provides a delightful mixture of cliff-top links with both parkland and heathland characteristics.

Website: www.caldygolfclub.co.uk
Email: golf@caldygolfclub.co.uk

Telephone: +44 (0) 151 625 5660

Par: 72 (White) / 74 (Red)
Length: 5,771yds–6,714yds
Type: Links/Parkland/Heathland

Fees:
● per round (Weekday & Weekend)

Tee-times are available to visitors – Monday, Thursday, Friday and Sunday.

Other courses in the area

Below is a further selection of terrific courses located along the north west coastline, and within easy driving distance of those already listed in this section.

● HESKETH GOLF CLUB

Originally formed in 1885 as Southport Golf Club, before a name change in 1902 in honour of the course landowner – Charles Hesketh Bibby Hesketh, and is, therefore, the oldest golf club in Southport.

Website: www.heskethgolfclub.co.uk
Email: assistant@heskethgolfclub.co.uk
Phone: +44 (0) 1704 536897

Par: 72 (White) / 74 (Red)
Length: 5,639yds–6,718yds
Type: Links

Fees:
● per round (Weekdays & Weekends)

Visitor Tee Times:

Monday to Friday	9.00 am-11.50 am / 1.40 pm onwards
Saturday	from 4.10 pm onwards
Sunday	11.00 am-11.50 am / 2.00 pm onwards

● DELAMERE FOREST GOLF CLUB

Originally designed by Herbert Fowler and about an hour's drive inland from the links courses along England's Golf Coast this classic heathland layout is well worth the detour.

Website: www.delameregolf.co.uk
Email: sec@delameregolf.co.uk
Phone: +44 (0) 1606 883800

Par: 72
Length: 5,496yds–6,588yds
Type: Heathland

Fees:
● per round (weekdays & weekends)

● ORMSKIRK GOLF CLUB

This charming, secluded, heathland course offers a departure from its links neighbours located nearby. Founded in 1899, Ormskirk Golf Club is based on the site of an old deer park; the course has hosted numerous regional Open qualifying events and is a fine test for golfers of all abilities.

Website: www.ormskirkgolfclub.com
Email: mail@ormskirkgolfclub.com
Phone: +44 (0) 1695 572227

Par: 70 (Blue/White/Yellow) / 73 (Red)
Length: 5,673yds–6,533yds
Type: Heathland

Fees:
● per round (Weekday & Sunday)
● per round (Saturday)

MIDLANDS & EAST ANGLIA

The Midlands

13

WOODHALL SPA, THE NATIONAL GOLF CENTRE – THE HOTCHKIN COURSE

The National Golf Centre,
The Broadway,
Woodhall Spa,
Lincolnshire,
LN10 6PU
www.woodhallspagolf.com
Phone: +44 (0) 1526 352511
Email: booking@woodhallspagolf.com

General course information –
Par: 73 (Blue/White) / 71 (Yellow) / 73 (Red)

S.S.S: 75 (Blue) / 74 (White) / 73 (Yellow) / 75 (Red)

Slope rating: 152 (Blue) / 151 (White) / 149 (Yellow/Red)

Length: 5,749yds–7,042yds

Longest hole: Par-5 9th, 461yds–583yds

Shortest hole: Par-3 5th, 105yds–142yds

Type: Heathland

Handicap Certificate: Required (maximum 24 for men and 36 for ladies)

Green fees – England Golf members*:
(Low season)
● per round

(High season)
● per round
● day rate / both courses

Non-England Golf members:
(Low season)
● per round

(High season)
● per round
● day rate / both courses

Juniors:
(Low season)
● per round

(High season)
● per round
● day rate / both courses

Price Guide: ● up to £49 | ● £50 – £99 | ● £100 – £149 | ● £150 – £200 | ● over £200

* = Members of an English golf club, affiliated to England Golf (98 per cent coverage in England). Bring your CDH Card or valid handicap certificate.

Caddies: Can be arranged by special request if booked in advance, +44 (0) 1526 352511

Equipment hire:
Three single seat buggies are available if required on medical grounds and should be booked in advance. Trolleys (both pull and electric) can be hired from the pro shop +44 (0) 1526 351831. Clubs also for hire (book in advance).

How do I book a round of golf?
The National Golf Centre at Woodhall Spa welcomes visitors at any time during the week and at weekends to play the Hotchkin Course. It is essential to book a tee-time in advance.

There are two ways to book a round of golf at The National Golf Centre, Woodhall Spa, via the Booking Office team:

Phone:
+44 (0) 1526 352511

Email:
booking@woodhallspagolf.com

HISTORY

How did Woodhall Spa, a picturesque, peaceful little village in the heart of Lincolnshire, become home to one of the world's most admired inland golf courses? It's an intriguing tale.

The village itself came into existence at the beginning of the nineteenth century rather by accident when a local coal prospector's mineshaft had to be abandoned due to rising spring water. Some years later, local landowner Thomas Hotchkin, had the water analysed to confirm its value before constructing spa baths and a hotel to attract tourists. Spa towns were very popular during the Victorian era and so it was for Woodhall Spa.

In 1902, the Hotchkin family offered a piece of their land, off the main Horncastle Road, to the local Woodhall Spa Golf Club in order to build an 18-hole course. The club, established in 1891, had already given up two previous sites to local property developers. On this occasion, it would most definitely be third time lucky.

Harry Vardon, six-time Open champion and member of the great triumvirate, was hired to design the new course layout. It would prove to be a very tricky assignment due largely to the terrain and abject weather conditions. However, the course was finally ready for play in April 1905.

In 1911, Harry Colt was brought in to make improvements to the original layout and make it a better test of golf. Colt's alterations resulted in a significant change to the routeing, which is how the course is played today.

By the 1920s, Stafford Hotchkin (or Colonel Hotchkin as he was then known, due to his service in the First World War) had developed a taste for course architecture and took it upon himself to take charge of any further alterations required. Upon his death in 1953, Colonel Hotchkin's son, Neil, would step into his shoes and was a passionate protector of his father's legacy.

In order to preserve the future of both the club and the course, Neil sold the facilities to the English Golf Union in 1995. Now known as The National Golf Centre, Woodhall Spa offers two 18-hole courses with the Bracken course opening in 1998. Substantial practice facilities were also built, which are now regarded as some of the finest in Europe.

After the Bracken was complete, the original 18-hole course was renamed the Hotchkin in honour of the family whose vision and dedication made this heathland treasure a reality.

Cavernous bunkers surround the green at the long, par-3 8th hole. *The National Golf Centre, Woodhall Spa*

PLAYING THE COURSE

The classic dilemma faced by all those entrusted as custodian of a heathland golf course: when Mother Nature, inevitably, begins to dictate the surroundings to a greater degree than was ever envisaged, yet everyone who plays there tells you it is one of the best examples of its kind, do you stick or twist?

The decision makers at Woodhall Spa chose the more courageous route and opted for the latter. In reality it wasn't a difficult choice at all – they wanted their old course back.

The result of three years' solid endeavour between 2016 and 2019, with Tom Doak at the helm, taking out huge swathes of trees, shrubs and gorse bushes, has seen this Lincolnshire gem restored to its original heathland roots.

The Hotchkin has always been a great course. Now it's better.

At just over 7,000yds from the back tees, this is a course that favours long, straight driving from the tee. If you're not a particularly long hitter, don't panic! Just focus on accuracy and craft your way round. The Hotchkin is famous for its deep, cavernous bunkers (142 in total). You may never know how good you are at playing in and out of sand traps until you've played a round of golf here.

After a gentle opening hole, the 2nd is a longer, more testing par-4 playing uphill towards a well-guarded green. Your tee-shot should aim for the wide section of the fairway just before a trio of bunkers on the right. Your approach needs to avoid bunkers both left and right front.

The 3rd, another par-4, is one of the course's signature holes bringing in to view the Tower-on-the-Moor, an iconic fifteenth-century monument now adopted as a symbol of the golf club. This is the only hole offering a blind tee-shot with the fairway hidden behind a bank of heather 100yds in front of the tee-box.

Hole 6 is the first par-5 requiring a fairly hefty carry from the tee to reach the start of the fairway (230yds from the back tees). The best line to take is along the right side toward a level green heavily protected by bunkers at the front. The 7th is a long dogleg-right, tempting you to be braver than you should. If in doubt, keep left of the trio of bunkers waiting to grab any wayward tee-shots.

The inward-9 starts with a short par-4 at the 10th designed to test your pitching skills. Your tee-shot needs to land short of the right-hand drive bunker leaving a pitch usually around 80–100yds towards a slightly elevated green making the flag appear closer than it actually is.

The par-3 12th hole is guarded on the left by the deepest bunker on the course.
The National Golf Centre, Woodhall Spa

The 12th is the third and final par-3 of the round and it can be pretty evil if your tee-shot isn't straight at the green. There is absolutely no room for error here as the putting surface is surrounded by some of the deepest bunkers on the course. Anything off line will almost certainly result in dropped shots.

The 17th may be one of the shortest par-4s on the course, but having a blast with your driver isn't recommended. Your tee-shot should aim left of the fairway bunker on the right to leave a pitch toward a green with pot bunkers waiting to catch anything pushed left.

(18) SIGNATURE HOLE: PAR-5 18TH, 395YDS–540YDS, (PAR-4, 442YDS FROM YELLOW TEES).

A great finishing hole usually playing into the wind. For your last tee-shot, try and give it as good a whack as you can. A longer drive will benefit from landing on the wider part of the fairway with the ideal line along the left. Bunkers line both sides of the fairway on this hole and can come into play for any shot towards the green.

Cross-bunkers straddle the 9th fairway blocking the route to the green.
The National Golf Centre, Woodhall Spa

Other courses on site

In addition to The Hotchkin, Woodhall Spa also has the following course available for visitors to play:

THE BRACKEN COURSE (18 HOLES)
Designed by Donald Steel, the Bracken is named after the wood where it was built. This parkland course perfectly complements the Hotchkin and offers an enticing, albeit less severe, challenge.

Par: 72
SSS: 73 (Blue) / 72 (White) / 70 (Yellow) / 72 (Red)
Length: 5,428yds–6,636yds

Green fees:
(Low season)
● per round (Adult & Juniors)
● per round (Adult – non-England Golf members)

(High season)
● per round / day rate (Adult)
● per round /day rate (Junior)
● day rate (Adult – non-England Golf members)

HOLLINWELL

Notts Golf Club Ltd,
Derby Road,
Kirkby in Ashfield,
Nottinghamshire,
NG17 7QR
www.hollinwell.co.uk
Phone: +44 (0) 1623 753225
Email: office@hollinwell.co.uk

General course information –
Par: 72 / 75 (Red)

S.S.S: 76 (Blue) / 75 (White) / 73 (Yellow) / 76 (Red)

Slope rating: 138 (Blue) / 135 (White/Yellow) / 143 (Red)

Length: 5,871yds–7,250yds

Longest hole: Par-5 6th, 453yds–582yds

Shortest hole: Par-3 9th, 108yds–178yds

Type: Heathland

Handicap Certificate: Required

Green fees:
(Low season)
● per round (Weekday / Sunday – pm)

(Shoulder season)
● per round
● full day (Weekday)
● per round (Sunday – pm)

(High season)
● per round / full day (Weekday)
● per round (Sunday)

Caddies: Not available.

Equipment hire:
Buggies and trolleys are available for hire from the pro shop, +44 (0) 1623 753087. Recommended to book buggies in advance, if required.

How do I book a round of golf?
Hollinwell welcomes visitors at all times during the week with the exception of Saturday and Friday & Sunday mornings.
　　There are three ways to book a round of golf at Hollinwell:

Online:
www.hollinwell.co.uk/Visitors/Green Fees

Phone:
+44 (0) 1623 753225

Email:
office@hollinwell.co.uk

Price Guide: ● up to £49 I ● £50 – £99 I ● £100 – £149 I ● £150 – £200 I ○ over £200

HISTORY

Tom Williamson's association as club professional with Notts Golf Club spanned an incredible fifty-four years. However, his introduction to the club, and to golf, was a rather inauspicious one.

At the age of 7, as he was walking home from school, Tom observed two gentlemen playing golf on a nearby common. After one of the men hit his ball onto a clearing, young Tom sprinted after it, picked it up and returned it to him. Rather than receiving what he thought would be a thank you, he got a severe telling off before being ordered to put the ball back where he found it. Later that day, the man saw Tom with his father and recounted the story to him for which Tom received yet another scolding.

The (Scottish) gentlemen Tom had encountered were John Harris and John Doleman, two of the original founders of Nottingham Golf Club, which had been established that same year (1887). A few days later, Tom caddied for Mr Harris, the man whose ball he had picked up, and they became lifelong friends.

Following its formation, club members initially played their golf at Queen's Walk recreation ground before moving to Bulwell Common in the same year.

View from behind the 2nd green with Robin Hood's Chair in the background.
kevinmurraygolfphotography.com

In 1899, a new site was found on the outskirts of Sherwood Forest near Kirkby. Designed by Willie Park Jr, the new course was opened in November 1901 and became known as Hollinwell.

The name Hollinwell derives from the Holy Leen well, which is situated on the course next to the 8th tee. Monks from the nearby Newstead Priory would stop and drink from the well while on their way to Kirkby. Founded by Henry II in 1170, it is now known as Newstead Abbey and famous as the ancestral home of poet, Lord Byron.

Hollinwell also has a proud association with Brian Waites who served as club professional between 1969–98, and is best known as the last club professional chosen to play in the Ryder Cup, in 1983. At 43 years of age, Brian was also the oldest player to ever be selected for the first time. Despite their best efforts, the European team would just miss out on victory, losing by a point: 14½ – 13½.

PLAYING THE COURSE

If you've never played golf at Hollinwell before, everyone who has will tell you that you should. Everyone is right. Everything you've heard is true. This is one of golf's finest walks.

Emerging from behind a promenade of pine trees, this sea of tranquility reveals itself in glorious fashion. Standing beneath the shadow of the clubhouse as you wait to tee-off, your first glimpse of the surrounding landscape merely whets the appetite for what lies ahead.

At its heart, Hollinwell is a heathland course. However, it also combines a rich blend of woodland and moorland topography as the routeing ebbs and flows up and around an expansive, tree-lined, terrain. The fast, springy turf helps to counter the overall length, propelling your ball forward along undulating fairways.

The road towards the clubhouse separates the first three holes from the rest of the course. The 1st is a fairly gentle opening par-4 albeit with a tricky approach towards a green guarded by bunkers left and right. The 2nd hole wraps itself around Robin Hood's Chair, a large rock to the left of the fairway steeped in local folklore where the legendary outlaw sat and surveyed his territory.

Perhaps appropriately, this is a hole that will definitely rob you of some shots to give to your scorecard if your drive isn't either straight down the middle or slightly right. From this position you still have a long approach towards a small, raised, green with a back to front slope and a bunker sitting on the right ready to catch anything pushed in that direction.

The 3rd hole is a medium length par-5 (par-4 from the red tees) bringing you back to the clubhouse. Straight hitting, avoiding fairway bunkers as you go, can be rewarded here, giving you an opportunity to claw back any shots dropped on the previous hole.

Hole 4 is the toughest on the course requiring accuracy off the tee to avoid the punishing fairway bunkers strategically placed for both short and long hitters. Any long approach shots skipping off the back of the green will land in penal rough; anything too short could find bunkers sat front left and right.

The 5th is the first of three par-3s and plays slightly downhill. Four bunkers line the left-hand side of the putting surface and should be avoided at all costs. There's plenty of room at the front of the green, so anything landing short can run onto the putting surface.

After the longest hole on the course at the par-5 6th and another tricky par-4 at the 7th, you reach Hollinwell's holy well beside the 8th tee – be sure to take a drink of the natural spring water as you walk by.

The back-9 begins with a quartet of superb golf holes, all providing a different challenge in their own right. This is Hollinwell's 'Amen Corner', spanning four holes rather than three.

The par-4 10th kicks things off with a demanding tee-shot that needs to carry a long stretch of rough with fairway bunkers on the left and out of bounds stretching all along the right. Your approach must fly all the way onto a raised green. Anything missing right will leave a difficult chip onto the putting surface.

Hole 11 tends to be a favourite among many who've played it and is one of the most picturesque holes on the course. Don't let the yardage fool you (360yds from the back), from the tee it is all uphill, so it looks – and plays – much longer. The tight fairway sits at the bottom of a valley, lined with banks of heather on either side. The green is well protected by a trio of bunkers at the front and thick rough at the back.

(13) SIGNATURE HOLE: PAR-3 13TH, 182YDS–241YDS.

After a long par-4 at the 12th, you reach the highest point of the course offering incredible views across the surrounding valley. The 13th is a fabulous, long par-3 all downhill. With the exception of one bunker at the front, short of the green, there is nothing hidden here; it's all laid out beneath your feet. Nothing long, nothing left, nothing right. Only straight down the middle will do.

Looking back down the fabulous 11th hole from behind the green.
kevinmurraygolfphotography.com

The 13th green basks in late evening sunshine at
Hollinwell. *kevinmurraygolfphotography.com*

Hole 15 is a tough, two-shot, par-4. Your drive needs to be straight and long to reach the deep valley running across the fairway beyond the bunkers at around 260yds. Steep banks on all sides and a solitary bunker, front-right, surround the green. Any approach needs to land firmly in the centre otherwise you may find your ball passing you on the way back down the hill.

The last par-5 at the 17th is fairly short but what it loses in yardage, it gains through the pure majesty of its setting as the clubhouse finally comes back into view. Lined by tall pine trees along the right-hand side, your drive needs to keep right to avoid two fairway bunkers on the left. Shorter hitters should lay up with their second shot in front of the valley to leave a pitch towards a green sitting on a plateau with three bunkers at the front and a severe slope at the back.

The tee-box at the 18th stares straight back down towards the clubhouse. A straight drive (aim slightly right of the clubhouse) should avoid bunkers either side of the fairway. There's room at the front of the green for your final approach to run up onto the putting surface.

The 18th green takes pride of place in front of the clubhouse. *kevinmurraygolfphotography.com*

18-hole courses nearby

● SHERWOOD FOREST GOLF CLUB

One of the oldest and finest heathland courses in England, originally designed by Harry Colt and enhanced by James Braid. Renowned for the quality of its greens and an extremely tough inward-9.

Website: www.sherwoodforestgolfclub.co.uk
Email: info@sherwoodforestgolfclub.co.uk
Phone: +44 (0) 1623 626689

Par: 70 / 71 (White/Yellow) / 73 (Red)
Length: 5640yds–6,806yds
Type: Heathland

Fees:
● per round

● CAVENDISH GOLF CLUB

Around an hour's drive northwest of Hollinwell, the course at Cavendish is regarded as being the most authentic of all Dr Alister MacKenzie's designs, remaining largely untouched since it was first laid down in 1925.

Website: www.cavendishgolfclub.com
Email: proshop@cavendishgolfclub.com
Phone: +44 (0) 1298 79708

Par: 68 / 72 (Red)
Length: 5,162yds–5,721yds
Type: Inland

Fees:
● per round

9-hole course

● CHARNWOOD FOREST GOLF CLUB

A thirty-minute drive down the M1 from Hollinwell, Charnwood Forest is a delightful 9-hole heathland course, designed by James Braid and built among the Hanging Stone Rocks, which dominate the surrounding landscape.

Website:
www.charnwoodforestgolfclub.com
Email: secretary@charnwoodforestgolfclub.com
Phone: +44 (0) 1509 890259

Par: 34 / 35 (Red)
Length: 2,648yds–3,014yds
Type: Heathland

Fees:
£18–£20* (9 holes)
£29–£32* (18 holes)
* = weekday/weekend

THE BELFRY HOTEL & RESORT – BRABAZON COURSE

The Belfry Hotel & Resort,
Lichfield Road,
Sutton Coldfield,
Warwickshire,
B76 9PR
www.thebelfry.co.uk
Phone: +44 (0) 1675 238600
Email: enquiries@thebelfry.com

General course information –

Par: 72 (Blue/White/Yellow) / 73 (Red)

S.S.S: 77 (Blue) / 75 (White) / 73 (Yellow) / 75 (Red)

Slope rating: 149 (Blue) / 145 (White) / 142 (Yellow) / 146 (Red)

Length: 5,755yds–7,255yds

Longest hole: Par-5 15th 566yds (Blue) / Par-5 17th, 469yds–564yds (Red-White)

Shortest hole: Par-3 7th, 116yds–177yds

Type: Parkland

Handicap Certificate: Not required

Green fees:
(Low season)
● per round

(High season)
● per round

Caddies: Not Available

Equipment hire:
Clubs, buggies and trolleys all available from the pro shop

How do I book a round of golf?
There are two ways to book a round of golf for the Brabazon Course at The Belfry:

Online:
www.thebelfry.com/golf/book-a-tee-time

Phone:
+44 (0) 1675 238600

HISTORY

The Belfry Hotel stands on a site originally occupied by a manor house dating back to the thirteenth century, which was used as a residence by the Knights Templar until their expulsion from England in 1277.

Ownership of the hotel changed hands on a number of occasions between 1959 and 1974, at which point the owners at the time – shipping company, Ellerman Lines – acquired some adjoining farmland with the aim of building two golf courses.

Peter Alliss and Dave Thomas were appointed as architects with the unenviable task of converting

Price Guide: ● up to £49 | ● £50 – £99 | ● £100 – £149 | ● £150 – £200 | ● over £200

fifteen potato fields into what would become known as the Brabazon and Derby courses, named after Lord Brabazon of Tara and the Earl of Derby – both former presidents of the Professional Golfer's Association. After three years construction, both courses were opened for play in 1977.

At around the same time, Alliss convinced the PGA to move their headquarters to new, purpose-built, offices at The Belfry. As part of this deal, the PGA agreed to hold two Ryder Cup tournaments at the Brabazon course within the next ten years.

In 1985, the PGA delivered on its promise. The Ryder Cup had been held firmly in America's hands since 1959. On this occasion, the USA ran into a determined European team, cheered on by a huge, expectant, crowd (attendance for the '85 tournament was 90,000 compared with 16,000 at Walton Heath in '81).

At the climax of a titanic contest, Sam Torrance etched his name into Ryder Cup folklore with a monumental 20ft putt for a birdie on the 18th green, handing Europe their first victory in nearly thirty years by a margin of 16½ – 11½.

The Belfry would host not one but three more Ryder Cup tournaments in 1989, 1993 and 2002. Overall, the Brabazon would prove to be a fairly happy hunting ground for Europe, retaining the trophy in '89, narrowly losing in '93 and regaining it in 2002 under Torrance's captaincy.

The 18th green at The Brabazon. Scene of Sam Torrance's finest hour both as Ryder Cup player and Captain. *The Belfry Hotel and Resort*

This time Paul McGinley created the iconic moment on the final hole, sinking the winning putt before jumping into the lake next to the green, sparking mass celebrations for the home team and its supporters.

The Belfry is the only venue to host the Ryder Cup on four separate occasions – a record unlikely to be challenged anytime soon.

PLAYING THE COURSE

There's a host of perfectly valid reasons why we may be attracted to playing a particular course. Sometimes, though, just being able to tread the same path as legends of the game is the only reason we'll ever need.

The Brabazon is a challenging golf course in its own right with tight fairways, shrewd bunker positioning, numerous water hazards (particularly for an inland course) and fast, undulating greens. But it has more than that. Something you can feel in your gut rather than see with your eyes.

Here, you don't just play a round of golf, you get to recreate some of the most iconic moments the game has ever produced. Can you drive the 10th like Seve? Can your 2-iron make it over the lake as straight and true as Christy's? Can you still hear the roar of the crowd as you sink your putt on the 18th green like Sam and Paul?

At the Brabazon, you get the chance to find out.

A water hazard follows you all the way along the left-hand side of the 6th fairway.
The Belfry Hotel and Resort

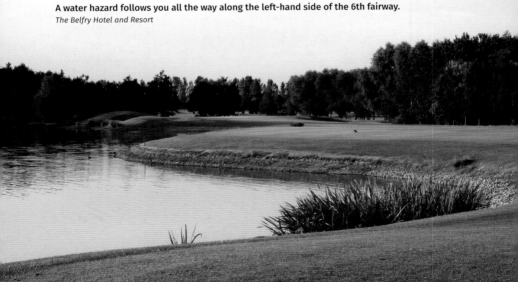

While it may be true to say most of the 'magic' happens on the way back in to the clubhouse, the front-9 has a number of challenging holes to test your game.

The opening two holes are both par-4s, which test your driving ability right from the start. The 1st has a cluster of intimidating bunkers in range from the tee. If you want to get off to a good start you need to miss the sand with your first swing.

At 379yds from the back tees, big hitters may be tempted to go straight for the putting surface at the 2nd, hoping to clear the river running across the front. With trees lining the right-hand side of the fairway, the wise move may be to lay up in front of the water hazard and leave a safer pitch onto a small, sloping green.

The 3rd is the first par-5, with bunkers along the left and right of the fairway, requiring a drive right down the centre. Another large water hazard stands between you and an undulating green. Only the longest hitters tend to make this in two, it may be best to leave the heroics for later in the round.

Of the trio of par-4s that follow, the 6th is the standout hole, regarded by Lee Westwood as one of the most demanding on the course. Water runs all along the left of the fairway right up to the putting surface, so aim right with your tee-shot and your approach. Be very happy with a four here.

Hole 7 is the first par-3 and the shortest hole on the course. From the tee, it can often look shorter than its yardage, which can leave a lot of under-hit shots rolling off the green into the water at the front.

The 8th is by far the hardest hole on the course. Your drive needs to clear a huge bunker and heavy rough along the right and water on the left. Missing the fairway will almost certainly result in dropped shots.

(10) SIGNATURE HOLE: PAR-4 10TH, 241YDS–311YDS.

After you close out the front-9 with another tough par-4, you reach the turn and the hole made famous by the late, great Severiano Ballesteros.

In 1978, during the Hennessy Cup (the first pro tournament held at the Brabazon), Seve watched his playing partner, Nick Faldo play it safe on this hole, hitting an iron onto the middle of the fairway. The Spaniard opted for a more cavalier approach, took out his driver and launched his ball high into the air, over the trees and water to land 8ft from the hole.

You may only play this hole once in your life so get out your big stick and give it all you've got because, well ... sometimes you just have to ask yourself: 'What would Seve do?'

The famous 10th green at The Brabazon.
The Belfry Hotel and Resort

Hole 12 is the longest par-3 (147yds–226yds), usually with the pin positioned on the back right of the green making it even harder to get close to. Trees surrounding the putting surface and a cascading river on the right create a real sense of an amphitheatre. The green slopes back to front so anything just short of the flag will leave an uphill putt and a great chance for a birdie.

After the tricky par-4 13th, you reach the final par-3 and the section of the course where Ryder Cup nostalgia begins to kick-in. The 14th is another hole where you're tempted to go for broke in the hope of emulating Faldo's hole-in-one in 1993. A two-tiered, angled green makes placement imperative if you're to succeed.

Once you've battled through the two longest holes at the 15th and 17th, you reach the climax of the round and the moment you've been waiting for. There's no finer example of a hole where the risk is so obvious, yet the reward so spectacular, backed up by the history it represents, than the 18th at the Brabazon.

In front of you, at the tee, you're faced with a large lake with a narrow fairway beyond. The further left you go, the closer you are for your approach. If you want to play safe, aim for the fairway bunker. You then need to land your second shot onto the famous, three-tiered, green before sinking that last putt and retire to the bar feeling like a champion.

Other courses on site

In addition to the Brabazon, The Belfry also has the following courses available for visitors to play:

● THE PGA NATIONAL

Opened in 1997 with the distinction of being the first PGA branded course in Europe. The course is set up to play hard and fast off the fairways with quick undulating greens offering an enjoyable inland links experience.

Par: 72 (Blue) / 71 (White) / 70 (Yellow) / 73 (Red)
S.S.S: Blue/74, White/72, Yellow/71, Red/74
Length: 5,735yds–7,053yds

Fees:
● per round

● THE DERBY

A parkland course offering a gentler challenge than its championship sibling with far-reaching views across the Warwickshire countryside and well-designed risk/reward holes.

Par: 70
S.S.S: 69
Length: 6,099yds

Fees:
● per round

To book a round for either The PGA National or The Derby course use the same contact details as outlined for the Brabazon.

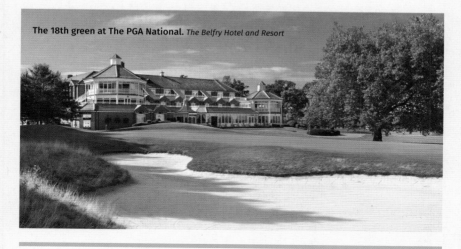

The 18th green at The PGA National. *The Belfry Hotel and Resort*

18-hole courses nearby

● LITTLE ASTON GOLF CLUB

Mature parkland course set within the grounds of Little Aston Hall estate. Designed in 1908 by Harry Vardon with further alterations made by Harry Colt a few years later and has largely remained unaltered since. Located just eight miles outside Birmingham city centre and a twenty-minute drive from The Belfry.

Website: www.littleastongolf.co.uk
Email: manager@littleastongolf.co.uk
Phone: +44 (0) 121 353 2942

Par: 72 / 74 (Red)
Length: 5,749yds–6,842yds
Type: Parkland

Fees:
● per round

● BEAU DESERT GOLF CLUB

Approximately thirty-minute drive from The Belfry, this heathland layout resides within the former estate of the Marquess of Anglesey. Originally designed by Herbert Fowler in 1911.

Website: www.bdgc.co.uk
Email: enquiries@bdgc.co.uk
Telephone: +44 (0) 1543 422626

Par: 70 / 72 (Red)
Length: 5,322yds–6,458yds
Type: Heathland

Fees:
● per round

9-hole course

● CHURCHILL & BLAKEDOWN GOLF CLUB

A true parkland test for all abilities, set among beautiful Worcestershire countryside.

Website: www.churchillblakedowngolfclub.co.uk
Email: admin@churchillblakedowngolfclub.co.uk
Phone: +44 (0) 1562 700454

Par: 36 / 37 (Red)
Length: 2,915yds–3,274yds
Type: Parkland

Fees:
£22.00 9 holes
£34.00 9 holes
(Lower rates apply for tee-times later in the day)

East Anglia

ROYAL WEST NORFOLK GOLF CLUB

Brancaster,
King's Lynn,
Norfolk,
PE31 8AX
www.rwngc.org
Phone: +44 (0) 1485 210087
Email: secretary@rwngc.org

General course information – Men:	
Par: 71	
S.S.S: 71	
Slope rating: 123 (White) / 121 (Yellow)	
Ladies:	
Par: 75	
S.S.S: 75	
Slope rating: 133	
Length: 5,882yds–6,457yds	
Longest hole: Par-5 8th, 494yds (White) / Par-5 7th, 456yds (Red)	
Shortest hole: Par-3 4th, 119yds–129yds	
Type: Links	

Handicap Certificate: Required
(28 for men / 36 for ladies)

Green fees:
(Low season)
● Singles per round
● Foursomes per round

(High season)
● Singles per round
● Foursomes per round

Caddies: Not available.

Equipment hire:
Four buggies are available and should be booked in advance. Clubs and trolleys can be hired from the pro shop +44 (0) 1485 210616.

How do I book a round of golf?
Royal West Norfolk welcomes visitors at all times from Monday to Friday only. Throughout the month of August, tee-times are reserved solely for members and their guests.

The preferred format for play at Royal West Norfolk is foursomes in the morning and 2-ball singles in the afternoon. Three and four-ball play is not permitted.

There are two ways to book a round of golf, via the Secretary's Office, for the links course at Royal West Norfolk:

Price Guide: ● up to £49 | ● £50 – £99 | ● £100 – £149 | ● £150 – £200 | ● over £200

Phone:
+44 (0) 1485 210087

Email:
secretary@rwngc.org

HISTORY

Holcombe Ingleby was a popular figure among peers in the House of Commons during his eight years as member of parliament for the Norfolk constituency of King's Lynn, also serving as the town's Mayor both prior to and immediately following his stint as an MP.

Originally a practising solicitor in London, Holcombe moved to Norfolk in the mid-1880s, through marriage. In late 1891, he took a walk with his brother, Herbert, down the beach road at Brancaster and came across a patch of land he described in the 1892–93 Golf Annual as 'a splendid stretch of strath, bounded by sandhills on the left and salt marsh on the right'.

Both avid golfers, Holcombe declared to Herbert 'Up clubs and at it'. Just a few months later, in 1892, The Brancaster Golf Club was formed. Ingleby took on the task of designing the course, assisted by Horace Hutchison (the club's first captain), however he would maintain very little work was required as the course was always there and he was simply lucky enough to be the one to find it.

The Memorial Gate, at the entrance to the course at Royal West Norfolk, lists the names of former members from the two affiliated clubs who died during both World Wars. *Steve Carr Golf*

While many clubs would dearly love to count a member of the royal family as one of their former captains, Royal West Norfolk has had four – the Duke of Gloucester, the Duke of Windsor and two Dukes of Kent. The club has also enjoyed 'Royal' status since outset when the Prince of Wales (later to become King Edward VII) accepted its invitation as patron.

Royal West Norfolk shares the links with Brancaster Village Golf Club, formed in 1894 as an artisan club with membership consisting of local Brancastrians (and nearby Brancaster Staithe) set up in order to comply with the original agreement recognising the site as common land. Since 1906, the two clubs have locked horns in a keenly contested annual match.

PLAYING THE COURSE

Many links courses around the UK can claim to be so near to the sea as to touch it, but only one is within such close proximity it becomes an island for a few hours each day.

Kicking sand out of your shoes is a practice typically undertaken after your round has concluded, yet there is such a place where you may feel the need to do this before reaching the 1st tee.

All golf courses are unique, some more so than others.

The links course at Royal West Norfolk resides at the end of a narrow road in the idyllic village of Brancaster, flanked by marshland on one side, a narrow strip of sand dunes along the other and the North Sea beyond.

When booking your round, be sure to check when the high tide is due if you're to avoid becoming marooned in the car park longer than envisaged. Although, as locations go, there are far worse places in the world to be left high and dry.

Brancaster feels like a long way from anywhere and the experience of playing here, at a golf course so at peace with its own solitude, is all the more joyous because of it.

View from the 1st tee as dawn breaks over Brancaster. *Steve Carr Golf*

Despite smart bunker locations and undulating fairways neutralising any big-hitter advantage, this course's best defence comes from Mother Nature, rather than anything man-made.

The average wind speed across most links courses in the UK is usually between 10–15mph; at Brancaster it's typically around 20mph and on many days throughout the year it blows much stronger.

If you want to know how good you are in conditions that regularly flirt along the parameters of playable, you need to come here. This is indigenous links golf in its purest form, on a course barely touched since it was 'found' over a century ago.

The walk from the Clubhouse to the 1st tee takes you across the opening to the beach and through the memorial gate, dedicated to the war dead of both Royal West Norfolk and Brancaster Village Golf Clubs.

You may need a moment to kick the sand out of your shoes before you commence your round. If the wind is howling, take solace in the fact it should be assisting you on the front-9 and only against you on the way back in.

The opening hole is quite a gentle start with a large fairway, shared with the 18th as you head back the other way. The best line off the tee is toward the 17th green in the distance. The fairway becomes more undulating and narrow as it moves toward the green – a regular feature across the course. Your approach needs to keep left toward the putting surface sitting into the dunes to avoid two bunkers waiting to catch anything pushed right.

The 9th green at high tide makes a difficult approach shot even harder. *Steve Carr Golf*

Hole 3 is a par-4 dogleg right with a clear risk/reward line off the tee over marshland. The safe line is toward two bushes sitting just right of a trio of fairway bunkers along the left. A tricky approach, toward a slightly raised green guarded by a ridge of sleeper bunkers (another common trait you'll see here), needs to aim straight at the centre.

The 4th hole is the first of four par-3s. At 129yds from the back tees, it looks straightforward. However, strong winds can create a dilemma over club selection. With three bunkers at the front and a raised green sat above a sleeper wall, the key here is not to be short.

The 5th fairway lies between the 4th green and the tee-box, therefore, keep an eye out for any golfers crossing your path before you take your swing.

8 SIGNATURE HOLE: **PAR-5 8TH, 443YDS–503YDS.**
Holes 7 and 8 are back-to-back par-5s. Of the two, the 8th is regarded as the most memorable and is the toughest hole on the course, particularly when the tide is in.

Stretched across two banks of marshland (which flood during high tide), an emphasis on shot placement is crucial. If you're going for the green with your second shot, aim for the left of the putting area.

Sailing boats behind the 9th green during high tide. *Steve Carr Golf*

The 9th hole, along with the 8th, changes complexion depending on the tide. The green here becomes an island during high-tide, making for a much more daunting approach shot over water. Try and keep to the right of the fairway with your tee-shot for the best line into the green. Your approach needs to aim left to be sure of keeping your ball on dry land.

The 13th is another dogleg to the right tempting big hitters to go straight for the green, which is well protected. Two bunkers sit on the right edge of the fairway ready to gobble up anything short. Safe rather than bold is usually the sensible approach here.

The 18th brings you back home across the shared fairway. Your final approach needs to navigate one last sleeper-faced bunker. A great opportunity to finish your round with a good score.

18-hole courses nearby

Approximately one hour's drive along the North Norfolk coast from Royal West Norfolk and Hunstanton you'll discover two of England's finest cliff-top courses.

● SHERINGHAM GOLF CLUB

Nestled in-between the cliff edge and the North Norfolk railway, which runs along the side of the course. A very challenging course – particularly when the wind blows – with incredible vistas from high above the sea.

Website: www.sheringhamgolfclub.co.uk
Email: gm@sheringhamgolfclub.co.uk
Telephone: +44 (0) 1263 823488

Par: 70 (Men's) / 75 (Ladies)
Length: 5,053yds–6,558yds
Type: Cliff-top

Fees:
● per round

● ROYAL CROMER GOLF CLUB

Established in 1881, residing 300ft above the coastline, the course was originally designed by Old Tom Morris. In 1905 Cromer hosted the first international golf match, which ultimately became the pre-cursor for The Curtis Cup some years later.

Website: www.royalcromergolfclub.com
Email: N/A
Telephone: +44 (0) 1263 512884

Par: 72 (White) / 71 (Yellow) / 74 (Red)
Length: 5,774yds–6,528yds
Type: Cliff-top

Fees:
● per round (high season)
● per round (low season)

HUNSTANTON GOLF CLUB

Golf Course Road,
Old Hunstanton,
Norfolk, PE36 6JQ
www.hunstantongolfclub.com
Phone: + 44 (0) 1485 532811
Email: secretary@
hunstantongolfclub.com

General course information –
Par: 72 (White / Yellow) / 75 (Red)

S.S.S: 73 (White) / 71 (Yellow) / 75 (Red)

Slope rating: 128 (White) / 123 (Yellow) /
133 (Red – Ladies) / 114 (Red – Men)

Length: 6,020yds–6,763yds

Longest hole: Par-5 2nd, 506yds–534yds

Shortest hole: Par-3 7th, 131yds–167yds

Type: Links

Handicap Certificate: Not required

Green fees:
(Low season)
● per round

(Shoulder season)
● per round

(High season)
● per round

Caddies: Not available

Equipment hire:
Clubs, buggies and trolleys can be
hired from the pro shop.

How do I book a round of golf?
Hunstanton welcomes visitors
at all times during the week to
play the championship links,
with the exception of Saturdays
(members only).

It is predominantly a
foursomes/2-ball singles course,
however four-balls are available
during the following times:

Tuesday
(from 9.00 am)   Four-balls
Monday, Wed–Fri
(from 9.30 am)   Foursomes/
                        2-ball singles
Sunday
(from 1.00 pm*)   Four-balls

* = during high season

There are two ways to book a round
of golf at Hunstanton Golf Club, via
the pro shop:

Phone:
+44 (0) 1485 532811

Email:
bookings@hunstantongolfclub.com

Price Guide: ● up to £49 | ● £50 – £99 | ● £100 – £149 | ● £150 – £200 | ● over £200

HISTORY

For any Harry Potter fanatics, the surname 'Lestrange' will likely conjure up notions of dark-arts wizardry from that notorious tribe of 'Death Eaters' devoted to their master, Lord Voldemort.

In Hunstanton, the Le Strange family enjoy a much loved and cherished connection with the North Norfolk seaside town stretching back over a thousand years. Arguably, the most famous member of the Le Strange clan – Roger – was deeply embroiled in the English Civil War (as a Royalist) and later became known as the 'Father of the English Press', after creating the country's first national newspaper, *The Public Intelligencer*.

In 1891, the Le Strange family gave their blessing for the creation of a golf course on an area of links land they owned in the Old Hunstanton village, overlooking The Wash. Initially, members of the Hunstanton Golf Club played over a rudimentary 9-hole layout, completed in just three weeks by architect, George Fernie. Hamon Le Strange was anointed inaugural Club President, investing £30 of his own money for the course construction.

In 1905, James Braid was drafted in to expand the course to 18 holes. Despite Braid's original design containing many more blind shots, in

View from behind the 18th green with beach huts along the side of the fairway at Hunstanton. *kevinmurraygolfphotography.com*

the main his layout is largely the one that exists today following minor alterations during the 1920s, and changes to the 17th and 18th in 1951 by Ken Cotton.

Over the last ten years, Martin Hawtree has also added his expertise, advising the course on a series of amendments, mainly focusing on re-bunkering around the 1st, 7th, 10th and 18th holes.

Of all the holes at Hunstanton, it is the par-3 16th that has the most famous story to tell. During his practice round at the Eastern Counties Foursomes in 1974, Leicestershire County's Bob Taylor recorded a hole-in-one. The day after, in competition, he did it again at the same hole. On the final round he completed the feat once more, again, at the 16th. Three 'aces' at the same hole on three consecutive days. An incredible accomplishment, surely never to be repeated.

PLAYING THE COURSE

On the northern tip of England's largest estuary, surrounded by a bleak, yet elegant wilderness of saltmarshes, mudflats and open water, a clubhouse sits proudly on top of a sand hill overlooking its golf course below.

From the moment you arrive at Hunstanton, you get the sense you're about to enjoy a classic links experience: 9 holes out, 9 holes back, separated by a range of sand dunes running straight down the middle of the course. Expect fast, undulating fairways peppered with cleverly located bunkers ready to catch your ball.

And then there's the wind ... any links course worth its sea-salt provides rather more than a stiff breeze as a natural defence and Hunstanton is no exception. Mainly behind you on the outward stretch, coming straight at you as you turn for home.

With most of the trouble to be found along the right-hand side, this is a course that tends to favour a right-to-left strategy from the tee and you get to test out this game plan at the opening hole.

At just 342yds from the white tees, the par-4 1st is not the longest hole, but the opening tee shot requires a steady hand if you're to clear the sand ridge in front of you and reach the fairway. Your approach also needs to avoid out of bounds along the right.

The par-5 2nd is the longest hole on the course. The tee-box is positioned to the left of the fairway, requiring another accurate drive to land clear of three bunkers just off the left of the fairway. Best to be short rather than long with your approach to avoid the ditch at the back of the green.

The 7th green surrounded by large sand dunes with the tee-box in the distance next to the trees.
kevinmurraygolfphotography.com

Hole 3, a long par-4, is the hardest on the course with the River Hun for company all along the right-hand side of the fairway. Any par-score here should be gratefully received. The 4th is the first of four par-3s, requiring a good shot right at the centre of the green to miss a swarm of bunkers surrounding it.

The 6th and 7th holes are, for many, the highlight of the front-9. At only 335yds from the back-tees, the 6th is a relatively short par-4. However, this hole – usually playing into the prevailing wind – is all about your approach shot, toward a raised, plateau green sloping back to front. Can you hold your ball on the putting surface? If not, dropped shots are an almost certainty. The wise move is to lay up with your second shot if you're not sure whether you can make it, leaving a pitch up onto the green.

The 7th is a classic par-3. Anything short will land in the large bunker at the front of the green, anything pushed right will fall off the sharp slope on that side of the putting surface.

10th fairway leading up to the green at the furthest boundary point of the course. *Hunstanton Golf Club*

The 8th and 9th holes are a rarity for a golf course – back-to-back par-5s. Your drive at the 8th should aim for the left-hand side of the fairway, landing before the public pathway, for the best line toward the green.

The 9th is the first hole across the line of sand dunes, moving in the opposite direction, back towards the clubhouse. Your tee-shot should aim for the lighthouse along the cliffs in the distance. This is a genuine three-shot par-5, toward a two-tiered green and the first hole of the round typically played directly into the wind.

The back-9 starts with a quartet of par-4s. The pick of the bunch is the 10th, bringing you right up to the boundary fence between the course and the coastline. Your approach shot here needs to keep left to avoid the deep bunker on the right of the green.

The final five holes at Hunstanton are among the finest closing stretches in links golf. Hole 14 is a long par-3 (219yds from the back tees) with a blind tee-shot over the sand ridge. Standing on the tee, it looks a longer, more imposing shot than it actually is. You have plenty of room over the sand ridge, which slopes down toward the green. Aim straight at the marker pole and you'll be fine.

Hole 15 is the final par-5. Pay no attention to the yardage (440yds–471yds), playing into the wind you'll need three good shots to make the green. Pay particular care to steer clear of the bunker guarding the right side of the green with your approach.

16 **SIGNATURE HOLE: PAR-3 16TH, 131YDS–189YDS.**
The most famous hole on the course thanks to Bob Taylor's amazing achievement in 1974 – three holes in one, three days in a row.

Usually played with the wind behind you, no less than seven bunkers swarm around the green. Can you emulate Bob's incredible feat? Take a deep breath and swing straight at the pin to find out.

The 16th green, surrounded by bunkers, scene of Bob Taylor's amazing triple hole-in-one.
Hunstanton Golf Club

The 17th and 18th are fabulous par-4s, providing a terrific final test as you march toward the clubhouse. The 17th fairway has a steep left-to-right slope; aim your tee-shot towards the top of the ridge on the left. The green is pretty narrow and sits on a raised shelf leaving very little margin for error with your approach.

You need one last, straight drive down the 18th fairway, missing the large bunker on the left. The green sits above the fairway and is now guarded by bunkers, making an already testing second shot even tougher. Make your final approach high and true to finish with a flourish. Anything on or near par deserves a well-earned drink in the clubhouse.

Steep, sloping fairway towards the 17th green. *Hunstanton Golf Club*

(18)

ROYAL WORLINGTON & NEWMARKET GOLF CLUB

Golf Links Road,
Worlington,
Bury St Edmunds,
Suffolk,
IP28 8SD
www.royalworlington.co.uk
Phone: +44 (0) 1638 717787
Email: secretary@royalworlington.co.uk

General course information –

Par: 70 (Blue/White) / 69 (Red)

S.S.S: 71 (Blue) / 69 (White) / 73 (Red)

Slope rating: 116 (Blue) / 113 (White) / 130 (Red)

Length: 6,242yds (18-holes)

Longest hole: Par-5 4th, 482yds

Shortest hole: Par-3 5th, 146yds

Type: Inland Links

Handicap Certificate: Required

Green fees:
● per round (18-holes)

All green fees are payable upon arrival behind the bar in the clubhouse.

Caddies: Not Available

Equipment hire:
Trolleys and buggies available.

How do I book a round of golf?
Royal Worlington & Newmarket welcomes visitors at all times during the week. It is predominantly a foursomes/2-ball singles course, however three and four ball golf is now available at certain times if booked in advance with the Secretary.

There are two ways to book a round of golf at Royal Worlington & Newmarket Golf Club:

Phone:
+44 (0) 1638 717787 / 712216

Email:
secretary@royalworlington.co.uk

HISTORY

Formed in 1893 and granted royal patronage two years later, Royal Worlington & Newmarket (often referred to as Mildenhall, after the small market town near to the course) is one of England's oldest golf clubs. It has also been home to the Cambridge University Golf Club for over 100 years.

Tom Dunn, following a request from the then landowner, Mr William Gardner, was the original architect

---

Price Guide: ● up to £49 | ● £50 – £99 | ● £100 – £149 | ● £150 – £200 | ● over £200

View from the 9th fairway looking towards the green and the clubhouse. *Kevin Diss Photography, www.kevindiss.com*

of the 9-hole course. Harry Colt (who, by chance, was the first Cambridge University Golf Club Captain in 1889) made detailed design recommendations for the whole course in 1920, which mainly included changes to the 3rd, 4th, 8th and 9th greens. Some were undertaken by the club but many were not. The course has remained largely untouched since.

Visitors to the course are encouraged, either before or after their round, to taste the delights of Royal Worlington's bespoke pink jug cocktail – synonymous with the club since members ran out of drinks at a party in 1934, creating their own concoction from the leftovers. A 'pink jug' consists of champagne, equal measures of brandy, Benedictine and Pimms, topped off with ice and lemon.

PLAYING THE COURSE

It should come as no real surprise that a course deemed worthy enough to be branded 'The Sacred Nine' by no less a golfing connoisseur as Bernard Darwin, tends to be the place where any discussion regarding the finest 9-hole course in the world usually begins and – for many – ends.

Part of the course's mystique is a tendency to lull golfers into a false sense of security, due largely to its fairly prosaic appearance upon first sight. Indeed, the 1st hole is a gentle, 482yd, par-5 that asks you to keep your drive and approach straight down the middle or slightly to the right for the best angle towards a large green.

By the end of the 2nd hole the realisation dawns that what may have appeared to be a rather 'cut and dry' round of golf is anything but. A par-3 at

224yds, aiming towards a small, upturned-saucer-shaped green, guarded by a bunker on one side and thick rough along the other. Playing this hole as a par-4 and chipping up to the putting surface is a wise move.

Hole 3 is a medium-length par-4 with a tee-shot played over the 2nd green and a large cross bunker that needs to be cleared in order to set up your approach. Try and keep your drive straight down the middle as the fairway is fairly rumpled and an uneven bounce can propel your ball into the rough.

5 **SIGNATURE HOLE: PAR-3 5TH, 154YDS.**
A hole that has dumbfounded many a fine golfer over the years and one that requires total focus and concentration from start to finish. Distance is not the issue here, nor bunkers – there aren't any. Attempting to hit the green from the tee has been compared to trying to land your ball atop a horse's saddle, so sharp are the drop-offs on either side. Only a putter held by the steadiest of hands will ensure a positive score at this devilishly tricky par-3.

Panoramic view from behind the signature 5th green. *Kevin Diss Photography, www.kevindiss.com*

The 6th is a strong par-4 (463yds). From the tee the fairway can seem quite a small target, sandwiched between tall trees along the right and two large bunkers on the left. The braver line is along the left to leave a more straightforward approach towards a raised green.

Hole 7 is the last par-3 and is less troublesome than the previous two. The 8th is another long par-4 and has a narrow fairway to aim at from the tee with trouble down either side. Your approach needs to clear a range of bunkers sitting around 100yds from the green. Anything pushed left could also find a large bunker protecting this side of the putting surface.

At only 328yds, the 9th is a short par-4 to finish and presents a final risk/reward challenge with a stream lurking along the right-hand side of the fairway, which doglegs left to right. The closer to the stream you are, the better angle for your approach towards the green.

18-hole courses nearby

● GOG MAGOG GOLF CLUB

Around thirty minutes drive down the A11 from Mildenhall, Gog Magog (named after the hills where the club is based) has two quite different golf courses available for visitors to play. The Old Course opened in 1901 and offers terrific views across Cambridgeshire (particularly from the 13th green). The Wandlebury Course opened in 1997 and is the longer layout of the two.

Website: www.gogmagog.co.uk
Email: secretary@gogmagog.co.uk
Telephone: +44 (0) 1223 247626

The Old Course:
Par: 72
Length: 5,642yds–6,735yds
Type: Downland

The Wandlebury Course:
Par: 70 / 71 (Red)
Length: 5,565yds–6,524yds
Type: Downland

Fees:
● per round
● twilight rate (after 4pm – high season)
(Both courses)

19

ALDEBURGH GOLF CLUB – THE CHAMPIONSHIP COURSE

Saxmundham Road,
Aldeburgh,
IP15 5PE
www.aldeburghgolfclub.co.uk
Phone: +44 (0) 1728 452890
Email: david.wybar@
aldeburghgolfclub.co.uk

General course information –
Men's Par: 68

SSS: 73 (Blue) / 72 (White) / 71 (Yellow) / 69 (Green) / 68 (Red) / 66 (Black)

Slope rating: 127 (Blue) / 126 (White) / 123 (Yellow) / 118 (Green/Red) 111 (Black)

Ladies Par: 74 (Yellow/Green/Red) / 70 (Black)

SSS: 76 (Yellow) / 75 (Green) / 74 (Red) / 71 (Black)

Slope rating: 139 (Yellow) / 136 (Green) / 132 (Red) / 119 (Black)

Length: 5,214yds–6,610yds

Longest hole: Par-4/5* 16th, 464yds–480yds

Shortest hole: Par-3 4th, 108yds–123yds

(* = 16th plays as a Ladies par-5 from yellow/green/red tees)

Type: Maritime heathland

Handicap Certificate: Not required

Green fees:
(Low & Shoulder season)
● per round

(High season)
● per round (Saturday)
● per round (Sun–Fri)

Twilight rate*:
● per round

* = after 3 pm during high season and 1 pm during low season.

Caddies: Not available

Equipment hire:
Clubs, buggies (with medical certificate) and trolleys can be hired from the pro shop. To book in advance call +44 (0) 1728 453309.

How do I book a round of golf?
Aldeburgh welcomes visitors at all times during the week after 11am. **The championship course is solely for 2-ball golf, either as singles or foursomes.**
There are two ways to book a round of golf for the championship course at Aldeburgh:

Phone:
+44 (0) 1728 453309

Email:
david.wybar@aldeburghgolfclub.co.uk

Price Guide: ● up to £49 | ● £50 – £99 | ● £100 – £149 | ● £150 – £200 | ● over £200

Looking down the 9th fairway towards the clubhouse. *Matthew Rose*

HISTORY

Golf's rapid expansion across England during the latter part of the Victorian era and into the twentieth century coincided with a turbulent epoch in British society as thousands of women made a stand against continued oppression to campaign for equal rights.

Elizabeth Garrett Anderson would emerge from this chaotic period as an inspirational figure and pioneer of the suffragette movement. In order to achieve her ambition and become Britain's first ever-qualified female doctor, Elizabeth would have to endure vast swathes of prejudice and hostility from her male peers. Among her many fine achievements, she would also establish the first medical school dedicated to female students and later become the first British woman elected as a town mayor (of Aldeburgh in 1908).

Elizabeth's husband, Skelton Anderson, was the main figure involved in the formation of Aldeburgh Golf Club in 1884. Skelton felt the open, sandy, heathland by the local railway station, overlooking the Alde estuary, was a perfect site for a golf course.

The original course design was a joint effort between John Thomson and Willie Fernie (fresh from his Open triumph at Musselburgh). In 1907, a change in ownership of the land leased by the club meant some major modifications were required. Another joint effort, this time between two Open champions – Willie Park Jr and J.H. Taylor – produced a series of changes that, more or less, provide the course layout as it is today.

In 1922, Harry Colt added his expert hand, mainly around the closing holes from the 14th onwards. More recently, Donald Steel altered the fairway bunkering in the early 1980s and in 2006, Ken Brown and Ken Moodie designed eight new tees and tighter bunkering to add length to the championship course and maintain the challenge for modern-day longer hitters.

Aldeburgh is very proud of its heritage as the first golf club in England (possibly even in the world) to offer women full membership and equal voting rights with total access to the course and clubhouse. There's no doubt the Garrett Anderson family were a major influence in this positive outcome.

PLAYING THE COURSE

If it looks like a heathland but smells like a links, it's a maritime heathland and there's no finer example than Aldeburgh. Here the distinct hue of heather and gorse blends effortlessly with the unmistakeable scent of a salty sea breeze wafting in from the coast.

Any visitors expecting a round of golf on an open, flat course, in keeping with Suffolk's surrounding topography, are in for a surprise. Aldeburgh takes full advantage of its hillside location, particularly on the front-9 with the 6th green the highest point on the course.

If the mere notion of placing your handicap score under the microscope keeps you awake at night or the thought of losing a few golf balls can be too much of an emotional burden to bear then this may not be the course for you.

If, on the other hand, you want to know how good you are at landing your ball onto tight, springy fairways towards firm, fast greens around a charming locale, then you've most definitely come to the right place.

The par-4 1st hole is a fairly gentle start with a downhill tee-shot toward a wide fairway. Aim right with your drive for the best angle toward the green. Your approach plays uphill, so take one club more than you need and aim right to avoid the deep hollow on the left.

Hole 3 can be played as either a long par-4 or a short par-5. Drive just to the right of centre to play away from a pair of fairway bunkers and to give the best line towards the green sitting slightly uphill from the fairway. Any approach aimed too far right could find the front bunker.

④ SIGNATURE HOLE: PAR-3 4TH, 108YDS–123YDS.
The shortest hole on the course, but highly likely to be the one that stays lodged in your memory at the end of your round. An extremely intimidating tee-shot toward a mammoth green sitting above the tee-box, surrounded by a long, sleeper-lined, bunker bordering almost the entire perimeter of the putting surface.

Beware the pin position as some locations carry far greater risk/reward than others. Anything landing below the hole should be safe and give the best chance for a good score; anything pushed too far to the edge will find the sand.

The raised 4th green with its long bunker ready to catch any mis-judged tee-shots. *Matthew Rose*

After the exploits of the 4th, take a moment to admire the gorgeous view from the 5th tee out towards the Alde estuary. This is a challenging par-4 (par-5 for ladies) requiring a tee-shot aimed to the left side of the fairway, leaving a mid-iron approach toward a green sloping away from you. With all the trouble at the back, a run onto the front right half of the green would be the sensible strategy.

After two more par-4s and a par-3, the front nine concludes with another impressive view from the 9th tee looking straight toward the clubhouse. The fairway is lined with bunkers either side of this hole making the journey to the green a perilous one. Best to play clever rather than bold here.

The 10th offers some relief for any wayward hitters with the widest fairway on the course. The 11th is not so forgiving and requires a strong, accurate drive to avoid the gorse along the right and bunkers along the left. Your second shot needs to navigate beyond the cross bunker and onto a deceptively sloping green – play towards the left edge to avoid a large bunker that guards the right half of the putting surface.

A tough closing stretch culminates with the longest hole on the course at the 16th, followed by a classic Colt short hole at 17. Still only a par-4 from the back tees, the 16th requires two huge hits to make it up the sloping fairway onto the green, navigating your way past both fairway and cross bunkers along the route.

Pay no attention to the stroke index for the 17th (S.I. 17). The final par-3 is a tough tee-shot, requiring plenty of elevation to land in the heart of the green and away from bunkers sat front right, tempting any player who hits a mean fade. A diagonal ridge running across the putting surface makes any attempt for birdie or par all the more difficult.

View from a fairway bunker with the 10th green in the distance. *Matthew Rose*

Other courses on site

In addition to the championship course, Aldeburgh Golf Club also has the following course available for visitors to play:

● RIVER COURSE

Part opened in 1973 before officially opening in 1975, the River Course is a perfect 9-hole companion for its older sibling across the road. Some of the course resides on what was part of the original layout for the championship course before the club was forced into re-routing it in 1907.

Despite having no bunkers anywhere on the course, some of the River Course's holes (in particular the 3rd, 4th and 6th) are regarded as equally challenging as those found on the championship course.

The River Course caters for both three and fourball golf. To book a round, simply follow the same process as outlined at the beginning of the chapter.

Par: 32 (9) / 64 (18)
Length: 1,959yds (9 holes)

Green fees:
£16.00 – high season
£12.00 – low season

18-hole courses nearby

● THORPENESS GOLF CLUB

Beautiful heathland course originally designed by James Braid, watched over by the unique 'House in the Clouds' landmark.

Website: www.thorpeness.co.uk
Telephone: +44 (0) 1728 452176

Par: 70
Length: 6,311yds
Type: Heathland

Fees:
● per round

● WOODBRIDGE GOLF CLUB

Provides both an 18-hole (Heath) and 9-hole (Forest) course, set in stunning heathland surroundings.

Website: www.woodbridge. intelligentgolf.co.uk
Email: info@woodbridgegolfclub.co.uk
Telephone: +44 (0) 1394 382038

Par: 70 / 73 (Red) – Heath Course / 35 – Forest Course
Length: 5,708yds–6,299yds / 3,191yds
Type: Heathland

Fees:
● per round (Heath)
£12.00 per round (Forest)

SOUTH EAST

WOBURN GOLF CLUB

Little Brickhill,
Milton Keynes,
MK17 9LJ
www.woburngolf.co.uk
Phone: +44 (0) 1908 370756
Email: golf.enquiries@woburn.co.uk

Green fees: Monday to Friday only by prior arrangement (subject to availability)
(Low season)
● per round*

(Shoulder season)
● per round*

* Includes breakfast on arrival, one course lunch and further complimentary golf, daylight permitting

(High season)
● one round package*
● two round package*

* Package prices are per person (based on parties of two to twelve) and include breakfast, refreshments and a two-course meal.

Handicap Certificate: Required (24 for men and 36 for ladies)

Caddies: Not available

Equipment hire:
Clubs, buggies and trolleys can be hired from the pro shop.

How do I book a round of golf?
Woburn welcomes visitors at all times from Monday to Friday, excluding Bank Holidays, to play the Duke's, Duchess and Marquess courses. There are no tee times available for visitors during the weekend.
  There are two ways to book a round of golf at Woburn Golf Club:

Phone:
+44 (0) 1908 626881

Email:
Courtney.Milburn@woburn.co.uk

Price Guide: ● up to £49 | ● £50 – £99 | ● £100 – £149 | ● £150 – £200 | ● over £200

HISTORY

For over a quarter of a century between 1978 and 2004, Alex Hay's dulcet tones soothed the airwaves during BBC's coverage of The Open Championship. Hay, with his mellow Scottish lilt, formed a delightful partnership alongside his colleague and lifelong friend, Peter Alliss.

Whereas Alliss brought the bravado, Hay provided the bonhomie while analysing and dissecting the performance of golf's greatest players as they fought for the right to be crowned Champion Golfer of the Year. Always so effortlessly assured and impeccably polite.

In 1977, a year before he first took up his position in the commentary box, Hay became the first resident professional at the newly formed Woburn Golf Club, establishing a lifelong bond that would see him become Managing Director between 1985 and 1998, Club Captain in 2000, and remain an honorary member until his passing in 2011.

In 1974, following agreement with Milton Keynes Development Corporation, the Marquess of Tavistock (later to become 14th Duke of Bedford) announced plans to build an 18-hole golf course among a patch of woodland, near Bow Brickhill Heath, within the grounds of The Woburn Estate.

The Duke's Course opened for play in July 1976, closely followed two years later by the Duchess', both designed by a former two-time Walker Cup Captain and respected architect, Charles Lawrie.

Woburn's affiliation with the British Masters began in 1979. Under the auspices of Alex Hay, the club held exclusive hosting rights for the tournament between 1985 and 1994, during which time such golfing luminaries as Ballesteros (twice), Trevino, Faldo, Lyle and Woosnam would emerge victorious. Both Faldo ('89) and Lyle ('88) won their titles in the same year as their Green Jacket triumphs at Augusta.

Construction work on The Marquess Course commenced in 1998, designed by Peter Alliss and Clive Clark, European Golf Design (Ross McMurray) and Alex Hay, opening for play in June 2000.

In more recent years Woburn has served as the home club for a number of tour professionals, most notably, five-time Ryder Cup winner, Ian Poulter, who has been the official touring professional for Woburn since 2003. Charley Hull joined Woburn as a junior member at the age of 11. In 2013 Charley became the first Woburn member to represent Europe in a Solheim Cup and has been ever-present in all three subsequent events (winning on two occasions).

The Women's British Open has been held at Woburn more times than any other host venue (eleven times in total, on both The Duke's (nine) and The Marquess' (two)), won most recently in 2019 by Hinako Shibuno.

The Duke's Course

General course information –

Par: 72 (White/Yellow) / 75 (Red)

S.S.S: 74 (White) / 72 (Yellow) / 76 (Red)

Slope rating: 136 (White) / 134 (Yellow) / 141 (Red)

Length: 6,065yds–6,971yds

Longest hole: Par-5 14th, 474yds–564yds

Shortest hole: Par-3 3rd, 121yds–134yds

Type: Woodland

PLAYING THE COURSE

If Woburn's position among the pantheon of great places to play golf is testament to anything, it's that glamorous cliff top locations or putting greens set against a backdrop of the ocean are not the only characteristics necessary – wonderful though they are – to create a modern course masterpiece.

Sometimes, a course (or three in this case) nestling within the tranquillity of mature woodland, each fairway intimately framed among the towering trees can be all that's required.

While many courses have made valiant attempts to replicate its splendour, there's nowhere in the world quite so Woburnesque than Woburn.

The Duke's course is the elder statesman of the three championship layouts available for you to choose from, and is a relentless examination of how accurately you can hit a golf ball. The smartest approach here, from tee to green, is to practice the fine art of target golf. Placing it, rather than blasting it, will serve you best.

The opening hole throws you in at the deep end; a long par-5 with out of bounds all along the left-hand side of the fairway. When the British Masters played here, Nick Faldo scored a nine on this hole (it actually played as the 18th during tournaments) so don't be too downhearted if you don't get off to the best of starts. If you can keep right along the fairway and avoid the two large bunkers at the front of the green, you have a chance of a good score.

(3) SIGNATURE HOLE: PAR-3 3RD, 121YDS–134YDS.

Walter Hagen used to preach that we should all 'stop off and smell the flowers' as we meander our way around a golf course. 'The Haig' could well have had this hole in mind at the time, particularly when the surrounding rhododendrons are in full bloom.

This beautiful par-3 hole, all downhill from the tee, is wonderful to look at but can be a real beast to play. Only 134yds from the back tees, but nothing less than straight down the centre will do. Anything pushed left or right will likely find the sand hazards either side of the green.

It is often said of the Duke's that if you can score well on the par-4s, you'll avoid any unnecessary damage to your handicap and the 4th hole is one of the most challenging on the course. A dogleg right to left, where its best to keep it right rather than cutting off the corner in order to leave the best angle into a two-tiered green.

View from the tee down towards the 3rd green on The Duke's Course. *Woburn Golf Club*

The next par-4 at the 7th is regarded as the toughest and a prime example of why accuracy, rather than length, is key around this course with out of bounds along the left of an extremely narrow fairway. There are only three bunkers on this hole and all surround the two-tiered green.

The 8th finally gives you room on the fairway and a chance to take a swing with a little more freedom than on previous holes, before the front-nine closes out with a pretty straightforward par-3 from a raised tee with just a large bunker on the left to keep away from.

Holes 10 (par-4) and 11 (par-5) are both fairly straight, gentle holes offering an opportunity to reclaim any lost shots from earlier in the round and before tougher holes on the closing stretch. The 12th is the last par-3 and, on first sight, also looks pretty uncomplicated. However, the green slopes back to front here so be mindful of taking an extra club than you think you need.

The 13th is a long par-4, which favours the right side of the fairway from the tee. Your approach needs to make it across a deep gully in order to reach the green. You need to aim left to avoid the drop off along the right of the fairway but anything pushed too far this side could find the bunker protecting the left side of the putting surface.

The Duchess Course

General course information –

Par: 72 (White/Yellow) / 74 (Red)	
S.S.S: 73 (White) / 72 (Yellow) / 75 (Red)	
Slope rating: 139 (White) / 136 (Yellow) / 136 (Red)	
Length: 5,801yds–6,555yds	
Longest hole: Par-5 4th, 494yds–504yds (Yellow-White) / Par-5 10th, 471yds (Red)	
Shortest hole: Par-3 16th, 121yds–149yds	
Type: Woodland	

The final four holes – all par-4s – have tight fairways but if you can keep your drives straight, you have a good opportunity to end your round on a high. Out of bounds again lingers along the left of the 15th fairway. Try and keep right with your drive from the 16th tee to give yourself the best angle into the green.

The 18th offers a rare risk/reward opportunity for the longer hitters. At 356yds from the back tees, a strong drive over the trees along the right could see you reach the green. If you'd prefer to be wise rather than bold, stick to the left and plot your way up to the putting surface.

PLAYING THE COURSE

In golfing parlance, The Duchess Course is the very dictionary definition of that most fabled term 'hidden gem'. There is a sense that it perhaps suffers from 'middle child syndrome', often viewed as sitting in the shadow of its more heralded siblings.

Its standing within Woburn's membership fraternity suggests a rather different tale, with many firmly placing the Duchess' as their favourite, among them Ryder Cup stalwart Ian Poulter, who said of this course: 'The Duchess' is Britain's best kept secret … anyone who can play here can play anywhere'.

If the Duke's course asks you to breathe in down the fairways, the Duchess' asks you to tighten your belt up yet another notch. This is a layout best described as one that must be handled with care. Anything slightly hooked or sliced off the tee will likely come to rest within the trees, but if you can keep your ball in play there are lots of solid scoring opportunities.

Adopting a more cautious approach will serve you well right at the start, where you're faced with a daunting opening drive at the 1st from a tee-box surrounded by imposing pine trees. Try and aim as far left as you can towards a slope in the middle of the fairway. Anything landing too far right and the slope will carry your ball into the rough.

All the par-3 holes on The Duchess' (there are four) can be placed firmly in a box marked 'challenging' and, with the exception of the 16th, they're all fairly long. The framing of the 2nd hole (185yds from the back tees) really gives you no option other than to hit your tee-shot straight and true towards a narrow green with three bunkers at the front ready to catch anything dropping short.

The par-4 5th hole is where you catch your first glimpse of the ancient Danish settlement, present on a number of holes on the course. Your drive should favour the left side of the fairway here to give you the best view into the green for your approach.

Hole 7 is another formidable par-3, providing clearer evidence of the ancient fortification as it forms a ridge cutting diagonally across the front left face of the putting surface. There's also a large bunker on the right to contend with. This is the longest par-3 and you should choose whichever club you need to make it all the way to the green.

The inward-9 starts with a long, straight par-5. Big hitters finally have a chance to make the green in two if they can keep their ball on the fairway from the tee. Holes 11 and 12 are two terrific par-4s. It's wise to stay right on the 11th fairway in order to set up the best approach line, avoiding a large bunker at the front left of the green. Hole 12 is a dogleg left where the recommended route is along the right, away from the corner.

The 15th is the last par-5 and dares you to take out your driver as the fairway moves uphill before coming back down towards a two-tiered green. Anything landing short of the top of the hill will leave a difficult, blind second shot.

17 **SIGNATURE HOLE: PAR-4 17TH, 327YDS–344YDS.**
'Local knowledge' from longstanding Woburn members would likely provide two pieces of sage advice for how best to play this dogleg left, short par-4. First – aim for the tall pine tree based on the right corner of the fairway with your tee-shot and second – keep your driver in the bag, it offers no advantage here.

Getting as close as you can to the pine tree will give you the best line into the green. A skilful, measured, approach will serve you well on this hole.

Behind the 10th green looking back down the tree-lined fairway on The Duchess Course.
Woburn Golf Club

The Marquess Course

General course information –

Par: 72 (Blue/White/Yellow) / 73 (Red)

S.S.S: 75 (Blue) / 73 (White) / 71 (Yellow) / 74 (Red)

Slope rating: 137 (Blue) / 133 (White) / 129 (Yellow) / 132 (Red)

Length: 5,832yds–7,218yds

Longest hole: Par-5 11th, 579yds (Blue) / Par-5 15th, 501yds–558yds (Red-White)

Shortest hole: Par-3 6th, 130yds–159yds

Type: Woodland

PLAYING THE COURSE

Bigger, wider, longer and with large undulating greens. The Marquess Course was built with the key purpose of moving Woburn seamlessly into the modern era, providing a layout more suited to the present-day demands of professional championship golf.

The Marquess' offers a number of subtle contrasts to its older siblings; the terrain is altogether more undulating with a richer variety of woodland surrounding the course and without the same level of intimacy as either the Duke's or Duchess', presenting a more open, parkland ambience.

Tricky approach towards the undulating 3rd green on The Marquess Course. *Woburn Golf Club*

Of the three courses on the property this is one where the driver is definitely most welcome, while still placing an emphasis on placement in order to score well. The Marquess' also provides lots of opportunity for anyone looking to practice their draw shot from the tee with several holes favouring a swing from right to left in order to set up the best approach towards the green.

As with many other modern courses, the Marquess' eases you into the round with a fairly gentle opening hole. Keep your drive to the right of the generous fairway, avoiding the large bunker on the left.

Holes 2 (par-5) and 3 (par-4) both slightly dogleg to the left with no real option to cut corners on either, so it's best to plot your way toward the green rather than try and fire your way through. Two bunkers near the 3rd green are further away than they first appear, therefore, be mindful of this when choosing clubs for your approach.

7 SIGNATURE HOLE: PAR-5 7TH, 454YDS–542YDS.

One of the most beautifully framed risk/reward par-5s you will see anywhere in the world, with a fairway split down the middle, separated by an array of stunning pine trees. So, do you go left or right?

If you opt for the right-hand side, you have a chance to go for the green with your second shot, however, this involves clearing a long gulley along this side of the fairway. If you go left, the landing area for your second shot is quite narrow and will leave a tricky third shot uphill towards the putting surface.

The outward-9 concludes with a long par-4. Try and keep right with your drive to avoid a large oak tree on the left, which will obscure the view for your approach if you land too close to it.

Hole 12 is a clever risk/reward par-4. At 343yds from the back tees, the green is reachable for big hitters, but you have to be sure you can clear the water hazards, otherwise the smart move may be to aim for the fairway island and leave a more straightforward approach.

The 15th is the final par-5 on the course and a favourite of Alex Hay who felt the view from the tee-box was one of the best he had witnessed. Playing into the prevailing wind this is typically a 3-shot hole for most.

The green is guarded by three bunkers on the front right making for a difficult approach shot.

The 18th, a long par-4 and last of a challenging stretch of closing holes needs a solid drive avoiding sand hazards strategically positioned both left and right. During construction of the course, a cluster of mustard gas mortar bombs were discovered just to the right of the tee-box here, left behind after the Second World War. The bombs had the exact same range as the yardage on this hole, so use them as your inspiration and give your drive one last big blast.

Your view from the 7th tee on The Marquess Course. Are you going left or right?
Woburn Golf Club

21

WEST SUSSEX GOLF CLUB

Golf Club Lane,
Wiggonholt,
Pulborough,
West Sussex,
RH20 2EN
www.westsussexgolf.co.uk
Phone: +44 (0) 1798 872563
Email: secretary@westsussexgolf.co.uk

General course information –
Par: 68 (White / Yellow) / 73 (Red)

S.S.S: 70 (White) / 69 (Yellow) / 73 (Red)

Slope rating: 121 (White) / 116 (Yellow) / 129 (Red)

Length: 5,582yds–6,265yds

Longest hole: Par-5 1st, 439yds–488yds

Shortest hole: Par-3 15th, 119yds–145yds

Type: Heathland

Handicap Certificate: Required

Green fees:
(Low season)
● per round / full day

(High season)
● per round / full day

Caddies: Not available through the club, but personal caddies are allowed.

Equipment hire:
Clubs, buggies (booked in advance) and trolleys can be hired from the pro shop.

How do I book a round of golf?
West Sussex Golf Club welcomes visitors at all times (either as guests of members or members of recognised golf clubs) during the week with the exception of Tuesday morning and all day Friday. **The conventional format for play is either foursomes or 2-ball singles.** An advance booking should be made via the pro shop. Available tee-times can be viewed in advance via 'Visitors tee-times' on the club website.

There are two ways to book a round of golf at West Sussex Golf Club:

Phone:
+44 (0) 1798 872426 (pro shop)

Email:
proshop@westsussexgolf.co.uk

Price Guide: ● up to £49 | ● £50 – £99 | ● £100 – £149 | ● £150 – £200 | ● over £200

HISTORY

Commander George Hillyard, during his tenure as secretary of the All England Lawn Tennis and Croquet Club from 1907 to 1925, had the unenviable task of moving the annual Wimbledon Championship from Worple Road to a brand new site on Church Road in 1922.

The new show court received a rather frosty reception and was viewed as a white elephant, which could spark a downturn in the tournament's popularity (the first tournament held there was plagued by rain every day). Almost a century on from that decision, it's hard to imagine tennis' prestige event being held anywhere else other than Centre Court.

After his spell at the forefront of one major sport concluded, Commander Hillyard channelled his energy into enjoying another – golf.

Hurston Place Farm (originally known as Hurston Warren, a huge marshland area covered in heather providing a perfect habitat for rabbits to flourish), was overlooked by Hillyard's home near Pulborough. It was this patch of sandy farmland that would ignite the Commander's desire to construct a new golf course.

However, despite Hillyard's enthusiasm and keen eye for land, generous financial benefactors would be required if this project were to become a reality. The West Sussex Golf Club would find theirs from within a local bridge society.

Two prominent members, Helen Ravenscroft and the Honourable Phillip Henderson, would provide vital fiscal backing by purchasing the Hurston Warren Farm Estate on behalf of the fledgling club and leasing back the land needed for both a course and clubhouse.

Behind the pristine 4th green looking back down the fairway at West Sussex.
kevinmurraygolfphotography.com

Of all the wonderfully framed holes at West Sussex, the par-3 15th takes some beating. *kevinmurraygolfphotography.com*

Without the continued support of both the Ravenscroft and Henderson families during a turbulent period (the depression era of early 1930s through to the Second World War), the club and course may not have survived.

Much of the endearing appeal of West Sussex lies in the fact very little of the course layout has changed from the initial design completed in September 1930 by esteemed architects Hutchison, Campbell and Hotchkin (known as the 'Three Majors' due to their distinguished military records and rank).

Other than modifications to the 6th hole (changed from a dogleg par-4 to a challenging par-3), the only significant difference between the 1930s and the present day is the prolific growth of the surrounding pine and birch trees. At West Sussex nature has been allowed to take its course and, as a result, created the most stunning landscape.

PLAYING THE COURSE

At the end of Golf Club Lane, on the northern tip of the glorious South Downs lies a course hidden away from everyday life, never yearning to be found yet offering nothing less than the utmost courtesy toward all who arrive. From the moment you leave, you'll be longing to return.

Bernard Darwin described West Sussex as 'a sandy jewel set in the Sussex clay'; Henry Longhurst suggested, 'man for once has done the right thing' when recounting his experience here.

What makes West Sussex so special is not just its majestic setting. A tough par score 68 is not the only reason it is so challenging nor the faultless bunker locations and heather-lined fairways ready to snatch your ball.

This course makes you ask yourself, in the most delightful way possible — how good am I at this game? A well routed, timeless test, with a layout stretching from one direction to the other. Upon first view it appears flat, but is surprisingly contoured and undulating, offering a delicious variety of holes as you weave your way around.

That variety starts right from the off with an opening par-5. It's actually quite a gentle opener with no real hidden dangers and a generous fairway. Stay to the right with both your tee-shot and approach to avoid any major drama.

The 2nd and 3rd holes ratchet up the tension and start to make you think about your shots. Members will tell you these are classic West Sussex holes. The ridge stretching across both fairways follows the path of an old Roman road long since consumed by nature. The tee-shot on the 3rd is fraught with danger as heather and bunkers lurk along the right of the fairway so best to stay left here.

The par-4 4th is a challenging dogleg left and a great warm up for what lies ahead, tempting you to take on the stretch of heather down the left-hand side. Be careful! It's much further than you think.

5 6 7

SIGNATURE HOLES: PAR-3 5TH, 134YDS–158YDS, PAR-3 6TH, 199YDS–226YDS, PAR-4 7TH, 391YDS–441YDS.

Holes 5 and 6 offer the rarity of back-to-back par-3s, both incredibly beautiful and offering very different tests off the tee. The 5th needs an accurate tee-shot to make it safely onto a green surrounded by mature pine trees at the back with bunkers and a sea of heather waiting to catch anything short. Anything right is sensible, anything left would be brave.

The 6th, originally a short dogleg left par-4, now the most memorable par-3 on the course with a tee-shot that is not for the faint of heart. Danger lurks along the left toward a narrow green with a severe back-to-front slope. Do you go straight for the pin or lay up along the right of the fairway? A par here deserves a pat on the back.

The fun continues at the 7th. Your tee-shot is blind over a hill with a large white sandy bunker that simply must be carried. There is no hiding place here, only a well-played shot will do. Trust the position of the marker post and either hit straight over it or slightly right. Anything left will likely be lost. This is the toughest test on the front nine and brings a superb close to a terrific trio of holes that will stay with you long after your round is over.

View from behind the 6th green looking back towards the tee-box. *kevinmurraygolfphotography.com*

Perceived wisdom suggests the back-9 is tougher than the front. The tee-shot at the 10th offers a genuine risk/reward target over the tall pine trees for the big hitters. The trip back toward the clubhouse really gets going at the 11th – the toughest hole on the course. The safe tee-shot needs to stay left to avoid fairway bunkers. Aim towards the left of the green with your approach to avoid a deep bunker covering the right-hand side.

Large bunkers and heather surround the 13th green. *kevinmurraygolfphotography.com*

Holes 14 and 16 are formidable par-4s and both have caused ruin to many a scorecard. It may not appear so from the tee at the 14th but you have more room down the left and this is where you need to aim your drive. There are many obstacles at this hole including a water hazard at the back-left of the green. Stay right with your approach to keep dry.

The stroke index (15) for the 16th hole belies its difficulty; pay no attention to it. A solid drive down the left is needed to reach a partially hidden plateau. Your approach must navigate a steep valley covered in heather toward a severely sloping green from back to front.

The 18th gives you a fine view toward the clubhouse. Your drive needs to be straight down the fairway to avoid heather and bunkers down either side. Take one more club than you think for your approach to clear the front bunkers covering a relatively flat final green.

The sun begins to rise over the 16th green. *kevinmurraygolfphotography.com*

18-hole courses nearby

● GOLF AT GOODWOOD – THE DOWNS COURSE

Perched high above the South Downs offering wonderful views of Chichester Cathedral and out towards the Isle of Wight. Revered golf architect, James Braid, designed the Downs Course in 1914. Officially a members only course, daily membership vouchers are available.

Website: www.goodwood.com
Email: golf@goodwood.com
Telephone: +44 (0) 1243 755016 / 755130

Par: 72
Length: 5,505yds–7,134yds
Type: Downland

Fees:
● per person*

* includes 18 holes at The Downs Course, use of practice facilities, meal and a drink in the clubhouse bar.

● HAM MANOR GOLF CLUB

Scenic parkland course designed by Harry Colt nestled between the West Sussex coast and the South Downs.

Website: www.hammanor.co.uk
Email: secretary@hammanor.co.uk
Telephone: +44 (0) 1903 783288

Par: 70 (White) / 69 (Yellow) / 74 (Red)
Length: 5,689yds–6,317yds
Type: Parkland

Fees:
● per round

● HILL BARN GOLF CLUB

Designed by renowned golf architect, Fred Hawtree. Offers stunning views over Worthing and out towards the Isle of Wight.

Website: www.hillbarngolf.com
Email: info@hillbarngolf.com
Telephone: +44 (0) 1903 237301

Par: 70 (White / Yellow) / 75 (Red)
Length: 5,717yds–6,229yds
Type: Parkland

Fees:
● per round

Surrey / Berkshire sandbelt

SWINLEY FOREST GOLF CLUB
Bodens Ride,
Coronation Road,
South Ascot,
Berkshire,
SL5 9LE
www.swinleyfgc.co.uk
Phone: +44 (0) 1344 620197
Email: golf@swinleyfgc.co.uk

General course information –
Par: 69 (Blue/White/Yellow) / 70 (Red)

S.S.S: 71 (Blue) / 69 (White/Yellow/Red)

Length: 4,956yds–6,431yds

Longest hole: Par-5 5th, 427yds–505yds
(Par-5 15th 510yds – Blue tees)

Shortest hole: Par-3 8th, 123yds–173yds
(Par-3 4th 109yds – Red tees)

Type: Heathland

Handicap Certificate: Not required

Green fees:
All green fees are confirmed by the
Club Secretary's office when booking
a round of golf

Caddies:
Must be booked in advance via the
pro shop +44 (0) 1344 295282

Equipment hire:
Clubs, buggies and trolleys can be
hired from the pro shop

How do I book a round of golf?
Swinley Forest welcomes visitors as
guests of members and a limited
number of groups, societies and
general visitors during the year by
prior appointment.

Bookings for a round of golf at
Swinley Forest Golf Club can only be
made via the Secretary's office:

Phone:
+44 (0) 1344 295283

Email:
golf@swinleyfgc.co.uk

HISTORY
Lord Stanley's round of golf at
Sunningdale had rather dragged
its heels on one particular day
making him ever so slightly late for
a luncheon meeting he was due
to attend with his boss nearby. No
problem; one would think any open-
minded employer should understand
such things can happen. Except the
precise location for his meeting was

Price Guide: ● up to £49 | ● £50 – £99 | ● £100 – £149 | ● £150 – £200 | ● over £200

Windsor Castle and his boss also happened to be everyone's boss – King Edward VII. His Majesty was not amused.

The king's displeasure culminated in him offering advice to the 17th Earl of Derby that perhaps a gentleman of his standing should consider owning his own course, where a more 'selective' members' list would avoid any unnecessary delays in the future.

The earl eventually heeded his monarch's advice when, some years later, in 1909 the king himself provided a plot of land within Windsor Great Park for Lord Stanley to establish Swinley Forest Golf Club. Three other Sunningdale members were drafted in to assist Stanley in his venture: renowned publisher Sir Hubert Longman and golf architect Harry Colt along with his colleague Alexander Davy.

Swinley Forest's almost mythical reputation was born from the founding members desire to have a Club shorn of most traditions so typical of golf establishments at the time.

Behind the severely sloping 4th green looking back towards the tee and the 5th fairway.
Graeme Roberts

A membership consisting of dukes, viscounts and field marshals are likely to look rather solemnly at the idea of taking on such a lowly rank of 'captain', which may explain why Swinley Forest has never had one. Nor has it ever had a handicap system or medal competitions, and up until the 1990s it did not even have official scorecards.

For the majority of its existence, Swinley Forest Golf Club has happily resided in what could only be described as self-imposed exile, surviving purely to provide its members with what they craved the most – peace and quiet in a small corner of England away from the madding crowd.

Up until recently, this endeavour had succeeded. Thankfully, Harry Colt made the utterly forgivable error of choosing Swinley Forest for his 'magnum opus', which can now be shared with a wider, eternally grateful, golf fraternity. Without ever trying, or more to the point – *wanting*, to ring its own bell, this hidden heathland gem is regarded as one of the finest of its kind.

PLAYING THE COURSE

In his own, typically, understated manner, Harry Colt suggested Swinley Forest to be his 'least bad course'. For the uninitiated, that means arguably the greatest course architect of the twentieth century held his efforts here in higher regard than any of his other illustrious designs, which include Royal Portrush, Muirfield and Royal Lytham.

Colt's mantra of allowing the land to dictate the routeing of a golf course was never truer than at Swinley Forest. The great legend of his work here, oft repeated, involved mapping out the entire course before one tree was felled (14,000 would be removed during construction).

At just over 6,400yds this is not a long course. However, the delicious variety of holes along with a low par-score of 69 (70 from the red tees) makes it appear much longer. The fairways are all pretty wide and naturally guarded by an abundance of heather. The forest that surrounds the course adds to the incredible vista without really interfering with play.

As one would expect with a Colt design, Swinley Forest's collection of heavenly par-3s (five in total) are often sighted as a highlight of the round, but it is the sloping, contoured and undulating greens that act as the main course defence.

After an opening trio of par-4s, the par-3 extravaganza starts at the 4th and Harry Colt's homage to the fabled 'Redan'. At just under 200yds from the back tees, the raised, left-to-right sloping green sits uphill and requires a full-pitched shot that may need one club more than you think.

The 5th is the longest hole on the course from all the tees except blue (15th – 510yds). Watch out for the pond sitting 140yds from the putting surface that can wreak havoc with your approach shot. The green has an aggressive back to front slope requiring careful navigation if you're to avoid 3-putting.

The 8th is the next par-3 challenge and the shortest hole on the course from all the tees except red (4th – 109yds). Missing the green off the back here will likely result in a drop shot so aim right for the centre.

The third par-3 is at the 10th and it's a monster – 223yds from the back tees towards a two-tier green protected by bunkers at the front and thick heather off the back.

While the quintet of par-3s are rightly held in high regard, they are not the only show in town at Swinley Forest which also boasts a joyous array of par-4s, none more so than at the 12th.

Behind the 13th tee-boxes looking back down the 12th fairway on the left. *Graeme Roberts*

This is a course that does not have signature holes, however the 12th is considered the most striking and dramatic at certain times of the year, particularly when the surrounding rhododendrons are in bloom. A precise drive needs to split the fairway to avoid bunkers either side, before an approach shot towards a green with a left-to-right downhill slope as well as multiple breaks. This hole doesn't give pars away very often.

The 17th is the last par-3 and toward another sloping green. By now you should know the drill – a tee-shot that needs to reach all the way to the putting surface and avoid rolling back. Anything short-right could land in the steepest bunker on the course.

The par-4 18th brings you back up the hill towards the clubhouse. Your drive needs to avoid the ditch at the front of the fairway. The green slopes back to front but try not to over compensate on your approach as anything too long could end up out of bounds.

The sun rises through the trees next to the 13th green at Swinley Forest. *Graeme Roberts*

SUNNINGDALE GOLF CLUB
Ridgemount Road,
Sunningdale,
Berkshire,
SL5 9RR
www.sunningdale-golfclub.co.uk
Phone: +44 (0) 1344 621681
Email: info@sunningdalegolfclub.co.uk

Green fees:
Both courses are usually unavailable for play from 1 January until the beginning of April and end of July – mid-August (check main website for dates).

(Low season)
● per round

(High season: beginning of April-end of October)
● per round (either New or Old course)
● play both courses same day

Emergency services tariff: (Police, Fire, Ambulance services and clergy)
● per round
● play both courses same day (during high season)

Handicap Certificate: Required (maximum handicap is 18 for men and 24 for ladies)

Caddies:
£80.00 per player per round. This fee **includes** gratuity and is paid in cash directly to the caddie. Must be booked in advance via caddiemaster +44 (0) 1344 620128.

Equipment hire:
Sunningdale is a non-buggy course. Buggies are only provided on medical grounds and must be driven by a caddie (total cost includes fee for buggy and caddie). Push trolleys and clubs for hire are available from the pro shop.

How do I book a round of golf?
Sunningdale welcomes visitors from Monday to Thursday (excluding Bank Holidays) throughout the season to play both the Old and New courses. Tee-times between 10.40 am – 12.30 pm are reserved for members on these days.

There are three ways to book a round of golf at Sunningdale Golf Club:

Online:
www.sunningdale-golfclub.co.uk/ Visitor Information/Green fees

Phone:
+44 (0) 1344 621681

Email:
info@sunningdalegolfclub.co.uk

Price Guide: ● up to £49 | ● £50 – £99 | ● £100 – £149 | ● £150 – £200 | ● over £200

HISTORY

Believe it or not, there was a time when building a golf course on land engulfed in heather and woodland was deemed nigh on impossible. The naysayers all believed the development of inland golf would never really catch on and it was best to stick to the coastline. Luckily, a man named Willie Park Jr felt differently, believing the duty of a golf architect was to practice the art of the possible.

If Willie Jr's childhood ambition was to become one of the most respected golf designer's of his, or any, generation, then he was certainly born in

Sunningdale's fabulous clubhouse sits in the shadow of the grand old oak tree.
Kevin Diss Photography, www.kevindiss.com

the right place, at the right time and, perhaps most importantly, in the right family.

As a boy, Musselburgh was Willie's playground. His father, Willie Park Sr (in 1860, 1863, 1866 and 1875) and his Uncle Mungo (in 1874) were both Champion Golfers of the Year. Willie Sr was, of course, the first ever winner of The Open and Willie Jr would add to the Park clan's victories with two wins himself (in 1887 and 1889).

This was the first golden era for golf and the Park family were at the heart of its expansion both in club making and course design.

At the end of the nineteenth century, Willie Jr worked full-time as an architect and was a man in his prime when two brothers – Tom (T.A.) & George (G.A.) Roberts paid him £3,800 to design a course on what had historically been used as farmland recently leased from St John's College, Cambridge in the leafy suburb of Sunningdale.

In 1901, just over a year after Park was hired, the Old Course (or simply 'the course' as it was known then) was ready for play. Over land initially considered unsuitable for golf (fourteen iron-age skeletons were excavated during construction), Willie Jr worked his magic and produced a fabulous heathland layout.

Park's architectural feat caught the attention of the first, newly appointed, secretary at Sunningdale – Harry Colt – who would go on to modify several of the holes and drastically alter many others throughout his tenure. By the time Colt left his secretarial role in 1913 many observers, including revered golf writer Bernard Darwin, felt his redesign had made an already terrific course even better.

In 1922, Colt and his protégé, John Morrison, were assigned the daunting task of building a new course using land purchased by the club on nearby Chobham Common. The aim of the New Course was to complement, not compete with, the existing course or, as it would now forever be known, the Old Course.

In 1934, Tom Simpson was hired to make a series of changes creating a clockwise loop layout. The new course was also given a name – Jubilee. Many influential members were unhappy at both the name and the changes Simpson made. One of the major gripes, allegedly, was the distance between the green and the next tee.

Colt and Morrison were reassigned in 1939 to reverse the loop and build new greens for the thirteenth and eighteenth holes. This redesigned layout of the New Course is largely the one that resides today.

Old Course

General course information –

Par: 70 (White / Yellow) / 74 (Red)

S.S.S: 71 (White) / 70 (Yellow) / 74 (Red)

Slope rating: 133 (White) / 128 (Yellow) / 141 (Red)

Length: 5,847yds–6,329yds

Longest hole: Par-5 1st, 477yds–492yds / Par-5 14th, 469yds (Red)

Shortest hole: Par-3 4th, 138yds–157yds

Type: Heathland

PLAYING THE COURSE

Upon arriving at Sunningdale for the very first time, whatever you know, or think you know, about this heathland paradise will almost certainly be rendered meaningless. From the moment you catch your first glimpse of the clubhouse beneath the shadow of the grand old oak tree you will quickly grasp that the reality is far, far better than you could have possibly imagined.

If you're travelling in search of golf's holy grail, there really aren't too many stops after here. This is a staggeringly beautiful place to play golf.

The first thing you'll note about the Old Course is its length. At 6,329yds from the white tees, it really isn't long at all. It's worth remembering the original course was designed by a former professional golfer, whose short game made him a champion and famously said, 'a man who can putt is a match for anyone'.

Your driver will not define how well you do here. Trying to blast your way around this magnificent layout is like attempting to clean the ceiling of the Sistine Chapel with a mop and bucket. The framing of every hole is utterly sublime, showing you exactly where your ball has to go. You'll enjoy your round a whole lot more if you listen to what the course is telling you.

'The Old' is generally regarded as being slightly friendlier from the tee than its younger sibling, making it more of a second-shot course. Almost all of the holes could be classed as 'half-par' – some higher, some lower.

This is clearly evident right from the off. The 1st is a fairly gentle par-5 that plays more like a par-4½. At 492yds from the white tees, longer hitters can make the green in two. Shorter hitters should aim right with their second shot just before the mound of heather at the end of the fairway for the best route toward the green.

The 2nd hole also plays like a par-4½, making it a real test for every player, particularly from the back tees. The ideal drive will land on the left of the fairway leaving an approach towards a dangerously sloping green protected by a bunker front-left.

Both courses come alive at the 5th, 6th and 7th holes. On the Old, all three are tricky par-4s of varying length and difficulty. The 5th has the oldest man-made water hazard anywhere (on a golf course) in the world. And it's definitely in play from the tee for the longer hitters.

The 7th starts with a demanding blind shot over sandy wasteland. Aim your tee-shot towards two trees along the left-hand side of the fairway that leave a v-shaped gap in the skyline between them and you'll be fine. Your approach is no less challenging from a sloping fairway toward a two-tiered green.

10 **SIGNATURE HOLE: PAR-4 10TH, 447YDS–453YDS.**
Take a moment to enjoy what you see from the elevated tee-box, the fairway laid out in front and the halfway hut sat waiting for you behind the green (the sandwiches on offer here are to die for). Use the stunning vista here as motivation for your tee-shot, which should aim left of the fairway as it shapes round to the right toward a slightly elevated green.

A hole that looks incredible both from the front and the back.

View from the 10th tee down the fairway on the Old Course. *Kevin Diss Photography, www.kevindiss.com*

Early morning sunshine over Sunningdale. *Kevin Diss Photography, www.kevindiss.com*

The 11th is a true gem of a hole, described by Fred Couples as the best par-4 in the world. Another blind tee shot over the marker post will ideally leave you with a short approach pitch toward the green. Missing the fairway will almost certainly mean missing your par.

The 15th is the last par-3 of the round and it's a long one. Don't be afraid to use your driver here, as your ball must make it past four bunkers protecting the front of the green.

From the 18th tee you can see both the clubhouse and oak tree in the distance. Aim slightly left with your drive toward the cross-fairway bunkers. Members would suggest using the clubhouse entrance as the line for your approach toward the middle of the green.

New Course

General course information –

Par: 70 (White / Yellow) / 75 (Red)

S.S.S: 72 (White) / 70 (Yellow) / 75 (Red)

Slope rating: 133 (White) / 127 (Yellow) / 140 (Red)

Length: 5,834yds–6,444yds

Longest hole: Par-5 13th, 510yds–516yds

Shortest hole: Par-3 2nd, 145yds–152yds

Type: Heathland

PLAYING THE COURSE

Sunningdale's reputation as home to, arguably, the finest twin set of 18-hole heathland courses anywhere in the world sparks the inevitable debate as to which layout is best. Is it the Old reliable or the New kid on the block?

The New Course is longer (marginally) than the Old and is generally regarded as a sterner test from tee to green. It is not quite as enclosed by woodland, so has a much more open feel to it providing a terrific panorama pretty much the whole way round.

The fairways on 'the New' are narrower and tighter placing a higher premium on accuracy from the tee requiring solid carries to ensure your ball isn't gobbled up by the heather or gorse.

Rather than length, Harry Colt used the short hole as his weapon of choice to examine a player's game. The five par-3s on the New Course are as fine a collection you will find anywhere. None of them will give up their par easily.

You don't have to wait too long to reach the first of the par-3 compilation, after a challenging opening hole, the 2nd is a captivating short hole with the green touching the horizon above the tee-box making distance much tougher to judge.

Better to land at the front where the green is wider than try and aim toward the back here.

5 SIGNATURE HOLE: **PAR-3 5TH, 152YDS–167YDS.**

As with its elder relative, the run of holes from the 5th, 6th and 7th on the New course are a real delight and will likely live longest in the memory bank.

The 5th is the 'pin-up' hole and a real Colt classic. Your tee-shot must navigate over heather and a large bunker at the front to reach a narrow, two-tiered green. Anything pushed right could find a bunker, left could find woodland. Choose your club wisely and just go straight at the centre.

A classic Colt hole. The par-3 5th on the New Course. *Kevin Diss Photography, www.kevindiss.com*

The view from the tee-box at the par-5 6th rivals the 10th on the Old for its beauty and is no less intimidating when the realisation kicks in that the fairway beneath you, flanked by heather on each side, demands nothing less than the surest drive. The two-tiered green is also well protected by bunkers and slopes back to front. A par here should be savoured.

After the front-9 finishes with a flurry of par-4s, the back-9 starts with a long par-3 at the 10th. The elevated tee may tempt you into the wrong club selection – don't make this mistake. The large, deep bunker sitting front-right awaits anything short.

The 11th (par-5 from the red tees) and 12th are a pair of tremendous par-4s. The 11th doglegs left, tempting you to cut off as much as you dare, needing a drive of more than 250yds to carry the whole corner. The green here is the narrowest on the course and requires a well-struck pitch to hold onto the surface.

The approach shot on the 12th plays uphill toward a green above eye level, making distance much trickier to assess. A bunker awaits anything missing too far right.

The final par-3 at the 17th is yet another typical Colt tester with the green sitting to the right of the tee and two bunkers waiting for any ball pushed too far in this direction. To be safe, aim front-centre.

View from behind the green back down the fairway at the stunning par-5 6th hole on the New Course. *Kevin Diss Photography, www.kevindiss.com*

Your round concludes with a fairly short par-5 giving you the opportunity to finish on a high and walk into the clubhouse with an extra spring in your step. Make your last drive straight and true; any approach should aim left, leaving a gentle pitch toward a green sloping heavily left to right.

18-hole courses nearby

● **SUNNINGDALE HEATH GOLF CLUB**

Next door to Sunningdale Golf Club and formerly the Sunningdale Ladies Golf Club. The late Queen Mother was club captain in 1932 and was patron for many years afterwards. The course is quite unique, measuring just 3,705yds and mainly consisting of par-3s, but is regarded as a real hidden jewel.

Website:
www.sunningdaleheathgolfclub.co.uk
Email: admin@
sunningdaleheathgolfclub.co.uk
Telephone: +44 (0) 1344 620507

Par: 58 (White) / 61 (Red)
Length: 3,705yds
Type: Heathland/Woodland

Fees:
● per round (weekday/weekend)

24

THE BERKSHIRE GOLF CLUB

Swinley Road,
Ascot,
Berkshire,
SL5 8AY
www.theberkshire.co.uk
Phone: +44 (0) 1344 621495
Email: golf@theberkshire.co.uk

Green fees:
(Low season)
● per round (Weekdays)
● per round (Weekend)

(High season)
● per round (Weekdays)
● per round (Weekends &
Public holidays)
● day ticket – one round per course
(Weekdays)

Handicap Certificate: Required
(maximum handicap is 18 for men
and 24 for ladies).

Caddies:
£60 per round. Paid in cash +
gratuity. Book in advance via Caddie
Master +44 (0) 1344 622627

Equipment hire:
Clubs, buggies and trolleys can be
hired from the pro shop +44 (0) 1344
622351

How do I book a round of golf?
The Berkshire welcomes visitors
at all times from Monday to Friday
throughout the year to play both
the Red and Blue courses by prior
arrangement. Tee-times are also
available on weekends and public
holidays after 12 pm.

There are two ways to book a round
of golf at The Berkshire Golf Club:

Phone:
+44 (0) 1344 621495

Email:
golf@theberkshire.co.uk

HISTORY

Herbert Fowler, architect for both
the Blue and Red courses at The
Berkshire Golf Club, was a late
bloomer to the sport where he
would leave such an indelible mark.
Regarded as a fine batsman in his
youth, cricket was more his game
where he played at first-class level
with both Essex and the MCC during
the 1870s before moving to Somerset
in 1882, even playing in the county's
first ever match.

In 1899, whilst in the midst of a
personal financial crisis, Fowler took
the advice of his brother-in-law,
Sir Henry Cosmo Bonsor (to whom
he owed most of his debt), and
decided to have a crack at designing
a golf course on a patch of heath
land owned by Bonsor at Walton

On the Hill in Surrey. The success of both the Old and New courses at Walton Heath would catapult Fowler into the consciousness of the golfing world and changed his life forever.

It's hard to imagine who can take more credit for the expansion of golf course design in England during its golden era than Herbert Fowler, and his twin layouts at The Berkshire, completed towards the end of his career (he was seventy-one years old at the time), are considered to be amongst his finest work.

Formed in 1928, The Berkshire Golf Club resides on land formerly used by Queen Anne for hunting during the late seventeenth/early eighteenth centuries. In 1916 the majority of the trees on the land were cleared to provide shuttering support for the trenches used during World War One. Afterwards, the army continued to utilise the area for training purposes. Both the Red and Blue courses were constructed at the same time, taking their names from those given to the opposing forces during military exercises.

The club has a long and proud affinity with many amateur competitions, regularly hosting the English Amateur Championships, the Women's Home Internationals and the Berkshire Trophy for Gentlemen. The latter competition can boast a winner's board including Peter Oosterhuis, Nick Faldo and Sandy Lyle.

The Red Course

General course information –

Par: 72 (White / Yellow) / 73 (Red)

S.S.S: 71 (White) / 70 (Yellow) / 74 (Red)

Slope rating: 131 (White) / 125 (Yellow) / 134 (Red)

Length: 5,696yds–6,452yds

Longest hole: Par-5 17th, 479yds–562yds

Shortest hole: Par-3 2nd, 128yds–147yds

Type: Heathland

PLAYING THE COURSE

As wonderful a sport as golf is, on occasion certain courses can produce a mundane feel about them when it's par-4 after par-4, with the odd par-3 here and there and a long par-5 every now and then. Thankfully, the Red course at The Berkshire offers no such chance, having a variety of par holes that can only be described as perfection.

Six par-3s, six par-4s and six par-5s; you simply cannot ask for a more splendid array, offering a fabulous blend of both risk/reward holes and plenty of opportunities to leave a positive mark on your scorecard. Each hole sits in glorious isolation from the others with heather-lined fairways surrounded by towering birch and sycamore trees.

Sitting on slightly higher ground than the Blue course, the Red course's terrain is also more undulating with quite dramatic elevation changes from tee to green. The distribution of the holes simply adds to the excitement with only the 11th and 12th offering respite with back-to-back par-4s.

The 1st throws you straight into the mix with a long par-5 (second longest hole on the course from the white and yellow tees). A pretty straight hole – straight and steady will serve you well on this course – but be mindful that any approach needs to negotiate a steeply tiered green, particularly if the pin position is towards the back.

'The Red' keeps you waiting until the 4th hole before you reach your first par-4. Regarded as the toughest hole from the white and yellow tees, your drive needs to keep on the left side of the fairway for the best line into the green. The approach should aim right to avoid a steep bank towards the left of the putting surface.

6 **SIGNATURE HOLE: PAR-4 6TH, 298-360YDS.**
A sharp dogleg-right, short par-4; the classic risk/reward hole, tempting you over the perilous tree line. The truly big hitters are advised to leave their drivers in the bag for this one. Anything too long could still end up in trees at the other end of the fairway. A perfect drive over the corner will leave you with a short chip towards a green marshalled by bunkers at the front, both left and right.

As you turn for home you're faced with a precarious par-3 at the 10th. Be sure to choose a club able to carry your tee-shot all the way to the green in order to avoid the steep bank along the right. Best to aim for the left of the putting surface, however, anything pushed too long will leave a tricky chip to save par.

Back-to-back par-4s follow at the 11th and 12th (the only back-to-back pars on the course). Both greens are within range for the longer hitters, but both play uphill with very little space to aim for from the tee. If you decide to play safe, be sure to choose your club wisely for what will be a steep approach up to the putting surface on each hole.

The 16th is the longest par-3 on the course at 221yds from the white tees and it needs nothing less than your best shot to make it all the way to the green. If you make it, the fun's not over as your putt can run very fast, particularly from back to front.

View from behind the green at the daunting par-3 10th on the Red Course. *kevinmurraygolfphotography.com*

Early morning dew across the Red Course's 11th fairway. *kevinmurraygolfphotography.com*

The longest par-3 is followed by the longest par-5 (and longest hole on the course). The 17th is a genuine three-shot hole to a green well protected by bunkers at the front.

The Blue Course

General course information –

Par: 71 – (White/Yellow), 72 – (Red/Blue)

S.S.S: 71 – (White), 70 – (Yellow), 74 – (Red)

Slope rating: 131 (White) / 124 (Yellow) / 136 (Red)

Length: 4,472yds–6,398yds

Longest hole: Par-5 6th, 438yds–526yds (Red-White) / Par-5 11th 394yds–465yds (Blue-Yellow)

Shortest hole: Par-3 4th, 86yds–153yds (Blue-White) / par-3 13th, 127yds–141yds (Red-Yellow)

Type: Heathland

Courses that start with a par-3 are rare; rarer still are those that close with one, as is the case on the Red course. The 18th is an uphill par-3 that usually needs a club more than you think. A heavily sloping green means your tee-shot needs to make it to the top to avoid dropping a shot right at the end.

PLAYING THE COURSE

Often regarded as the less 'senior' of the two Berkshire courses, and doesn't replicate the 'perfect' mixture of par holes on the Red. Nevertheless many who have played the Blue course regard it as tougher than its sibling (it is also much flatter) and right from the start of your round you will immediately understand why.

---

1 **SIGNATURE HOLE: PAR-3 1ST, 104YDS–217YDS.**

Any course that greets you with an opening long par-3 needs to be taken seriously. Between you and the raised 1st green lies a sea of beautiful heather. Your tee-shot needs to be all carry (front-left is ideal), but anything too long could also find trouble. The throng of members looking on from the clubhouse compounds the adrenalin and theatre of this fabulous 1st hole. Just relax and make your swing straight and true.

After the drama of the 1st hole, the rest of the front-9 takes a more genteel approach, with a number of good scoring opportunities to claw back any nightmare opening scenarios. The par-4 2nd offers instant payback if you keep your drive down the right of the fairway toward a small green guarded by three bunkers front and right.

View from the 1st green on the Blue Course, played in full view of the clubhouse.
kevinmurraygolfphotography.com

Large bunker protects the 9th green on the Blue Course.
kevinmurraygolfphotography.com

Both par-5s (3rd and 6th holes) offer further chances to make a positive mark on your scorecard if you can keep your drive straight down the middle. The opening-9 closes with another short par-4 at only 310yds from the back tees. A driver here may not be the best choice, unless you're confident of making it all the way, as the fairway narrows and slopes uphill toward the green, guarded by a large bunker front-right.

The back-9 finishes with a set of five demanding par-4s starting with a blind tee-shot on the 14th. So blind, in fact, that it would be ill advised to use a driver here as the fairway begins to narrow quite sharply after 200yds. Anything pushed too far right will be blocked by the tree line.

The 16th is regarded as the hardest of the closing quintet. A slight dogleg-left, your drive needs to navigate around a fairway bunker on the corner of the dogleg. Take an extra club for your approach towards an uphill green with a severe slope from back to front and left to right. Don't be too downhearted with a bogey score here and a par should be cherished.

If you ever have the pleasure of spending a day at the Berkshire Golf Club to play both these fine courses (the carvery lunch is a particular delight and highly recommended), perceived wisdom amongst those who have played them suggests starting with the Red course followed by the Blue, if only to get yourself warmed up for the 1st tee shot beneath the shadow of the clubhouse.

The fairway weaves its way towards the green at the 11th hole on the Blue Course.
kevinmurraygolfphotography.com

25

ST GEORGE'S HILL GOLF CLUB – RED & BLUE COURSE

Golf Club Road,
St George's Hill,
Weybridge,
Surrey
KT13 0NL
stgeorgeshillgolfclub.co.uk
Phone: +44 (0) 1932 847758
Email: admin@stgeorgeshillgolfclub.co.uk

General course information –
Par: 70 (White/Yellow) / 72 (Red)

S.S.S: 72 (White) / 71 (Yellow) / 72 (Red)

Slope rating: 136 (White) / 135 (Yellow) / 128 (Red)

Length: 5,519yds-6,581yds

Longest hole: Par-5 15th, 483yds–547yds

Shortest hole: Par-3 11th, 102yds–119yds

Type: Heathland

Handicap Certificate: Not required

(Periodic checks may be made to verify golfing ability in the interests of maintaining the pace of play on the course)

Green fees:
(*Low season)
● per round (18 or 27-holes)
● 36-holes

(High season)
● per round (18-holes)
● per round (27 or 36-holes)

(* = Either the Red or Blue course is typically closed during Jan/Feb for maintenance, therefore the 18-hole combination would be either Red & Green or Blue & Green during this period)

Caddies:
Must be booked in advance via the caddiemaster, +44 (0) 1932 858175

Equipment hire:
Buggies (booked in advance) and trolleys can be hired from the pro shop, + 44 (0) 1932 843523

How do I book a round of golf?
St George's Hill welcomes visitors at the following times during the week:
   2-ball singles/foursomes:
Wednesday & Thursday (afternoons only)
   3 or 4 balls:
Wednesday & Thursday (morning and afternoon), Friday (morning only)
   In addition there is occasional availability on Monday and Tuesday afternoons (excluding bank holidays). Course bookings are not typically available during the Christmas/New Year period.
   There are two ways to book a round of golf at St George's Hill Golf Club:

Price Guide: ● up to £49 | ● £50 – £99 | ● £100 – £149 | ● £150 – £200 | ● over £200

Phone:
+44 (0) 1932 847758

Email:
admin@stgeorgeshillgolfclub.co.uk

HISTORY

Walter George (W.G.) Tarrant was a rather imposing figure. Standing over 6ft tall, with a thick beard, he was thought to have a striking resemblance to King Edward VII. Known as a man of vision and enterprise, Surrey's 'master builder' and developer would, in 1911, turn his attention to an area of woodland on the Ellesmere estate, near Weybridge transforming it into a thriving residential community with state-of-the-art sporting facilities.

The plans also included construction of a championship golf course, where Tarrant, once again, provided shrewd foresight by appointing an architect who was at the top of his game – Harry S. Colt. Fresh from his recent successes in the area with both Sunningdale and Swinley Forest, Colt set to work on what many believe to be his finest creation.

On the 2nd October 1913 St George's Hill golf course was opened for play by Prince Alexander of Teck (brother-in-law to King George V and first

View from behind the 1st green on the Red course with the clubhouse in the distance.
kevinmurraygolfphotography.com

president of the club). Some leading professionals of the day were also present to compete in the inaugural match, including Open champions James Braid and J.H. Taylor. Former amateur champion Horace Hutchinson was elected as the first captain and Frank Frostick was appointed the first club professional (a position he would hold for nearly forty years until his retirement in 1952, replaced by Max Faulkner, 1951 Open champion).

Only a year after the club's formation, war would be declared during which time the clubhouse was commandeered by the Red Cross and converted into a military hospital, treating over 3,000 wounded during the conflict. A fire in 1920 reduced the clubhouse to a shell, destroying the original thatched roof. The re-designed building – this time with a flat roof – opened a few years later and is the grand design sat high above the course that greets you today. After the outbreak of the Second World War, the course would again be acquired for military purposes. This time as a site for barrage balloons, placed on the 5th, 7th and 17th holes as a defence for the nearby Vickers aircraft factory.

In 1929 a second 18-hole course was commissioned in order to attract new members and, again, Harry Colt would be called upon to design the new layout. By 1946, due to a lack of funding and falling membership as a result of the war, the new course was reduced from 18 to 9 holes. In 1987 the second course (now known as the Green course) would receive a timely redesign by Donald Steel, following plans submitted by club member, Peter Preston.

This 27-hole layout is the one that resides today, consisting of three loops of 9-holes – Red, Blue and Green - with the Red & Blue courses traditionally recognised as the championship 18-hole combination.

PLAYING THE COURSE

Harry Colt was once quoted as saying: 'The only means whereby an attractive piece of ground can be turned into a satisfying golf course is to work to the natural features of the site in question.' Of all his feats of architectural wonder spread across the world, these words could never be more accurate than for Colt's heathland tour de force at St George's Hill.

Painstakingly carved out of 900 acres of woodland and heather, for many who have played here, St George's Hill is the unheralded hero of the Surrey/Berkshire sandbelt. Too polite, perhaps, to shout about its many attributes, but nevertheless providing you, upon arrival, with a sense you're about to play a very special round of golf.

Before you head out, take a moment to assess the stunning panorama from the unique vantage point of the promenade in front of the clubhouse. The sweeping, undulating, terrain here is unlike any other in the area.

What becomes immediately clear is the master designer made good on his words, weaving his creative magic to quite dramatic effect.

The Red/Blue course is laid out in a figure of eight with the 1st tee, 9th green, 10th tee and 18th green all situated below the clubhouse. Both the 1st and 10th tees sit back-to-back, with only a path to separate them.

Starting at the Red-9, the sense of anticipation continues from the elevated 1st tee looking down towards the fairway beneath you. A solid drive is needed on this tough opening par-4, avoiding two bunkers on the left. Your approach plays uphill and generally requires one club more than you may think towards a green guarded by two bunkers front-right.

Another difficult par-4 follows at the 2nd before the first of four fabulous par-3s (would you expect anything less from a Colt design?). At 198yds from the white tees but from an elevated position, the hole may not play quite as long as the distance suggests. A tricky green to hit, protected by bunkers at the front.

After three more par-4s, the 7th is the only par-5 on the Red-9. At only 476yds from the back tees, it offers a good chance to take back some shots, particularly for longer hitters, however a fairway bunker sitting at 290yds could catch any booming drives. The green is in range and relatively flat but surrounded by bunkers on all sides, making it a tough reach in two.

8   **SIGNATURE HOLE: PAR-3 8TH, 151YDS–179YDS.**
The doyen of the short hole saved one of his best (and, arguably, his most beautiful) motifs for the 8th at St George's Hill. A steep valley sits between you and an inverted green, which gently slopes towards the front.

Bunkers lie in wait at the front of the green and whilst they really shouldn't be in play, they so often are, catching lots of nervously hit tee-shots. Beware anything hit too long to over compensate as thick rough off the back of the putting surface will also put paid to any dreams of a good score.

The opening hole on the Blue-9, as with the Red-9, is another challenging par-4 and is often played into the wind. Your drive is semi-blind, so use the tall standalone pine tree in the distance as your marker. Often played as a par-5, your approach to the large, two-tiered green should aim left of the flag. A par score here deserves a pat on the back.

View from the tee looking towards the 8th green, Red course. *kevinmurraygolfphotography.com*

A short par-3 at the 11th is followed by two more testing par-4s at the 12th and 13th. The 14th is the final par-3 on the Red & Blue course combination and, at over 200yds from the back tees, is regarded as the most demanding. A pond lies short of the green and a large bunker sits front-left. Any tee-shot landing short will likely roll back down the slope and find trouble. If you've already had a pat on the back at the 10th, give yourself a high-five if you secure the same score here.

The 15th is the longest hole on the course and this par-5 is an exercise in how straight you can drive a golf ball. Hit it straight and you can score well here. The large green has two bunkers sitting at the front protecting it from anyone going for a long second shot. A 3-shot strategy may be more sensible.

The final three holes on the Blue-9 are all difficult par-4s. The 18th brings you back to the foot of the clubhouse. Use the flag on the 9th green as your marker for your drive here, aiming to the left of the fairway. Your approach is uphill and may, again, need one club more than you envisage (a good rule of thumb around this course). The green has a severe slope from right to left. Any putts hit too hard above the hole could roll into the bunkers beyond, so a deft hand is required to avoid any embarrassments right at the end.

Looking towards the green on the par-4 12th hole, Blue course. *kevinmurraygolfphotography.com*

A final uphill approach for glory on the 18th, Blue course. *kevinmurraygolfphotography.com*

Other courses on site

In addition to the Red & Blue course, St George's Hill also has an additional 9-hole course available, as previously mentioned in this chapter, which visitors can play as part of an alternative 18-hole combination with either of the aforementioned layouts.

● GREEN COURSE

The Green course consists of the remaining 9-holes from the original second course constructed by Harry Colt in 1929. Despite being the shortest of the three 9-hole courses it is regarded as a favourite among many members and regular visitors. It is also viewed by some as a slightly tougher test, despite its length, consisting of tighter fairways and difficult green positions. Recent redevelopments to the Green's layout have further enhanced its reputation as a worthy adversary to its course siblings.

To book a round for the Green course visitors should use the same booking procedure as the Red/Blue course.

Par: 35 (9-holes)
Length: 2,952yds

Green fees:
As outlined at the beginning of the chapter.

Looking back down the fairway from behind the green on the closing hole, Green course. *kevinmurraygolfphotography.com*

WALTON HEATH GOLF CLUB

Walton on the Hill,
Tadworth,
KT20 7TP
www.waltonheath.com
Phone: +44 (0) 1737 812060/812380
Email: secretary@waltonheath.com

Green fees:
(Low season)
- per round / ● two rounds (Weekdays)
- per round (Weekends & Public Holidays)

(High season)
- per round / ● two rounds (Weekdays)
- per round (Weekends & Public Holidays)

Handicap Certificate: Not required

Caddies:
£60.00 per player per round. Caddie fees to be paid in cash (+ gratuity). Book in advance via caddiemaster +44 (0) 7810 576607.

Equipment hire:
Clubs and trolleys can be hired from the pro shop +44 (0) 1737 812152. A small number of buggies are available if required on medical grounds and must be booked in advance via reception +44 (0) 1737 812060.

How do I book a round of golf?

Walton Heath welcomes visitors at all times during the week after 9.30 am and after midday on weekends & public holidays to play both the Old and New course.

There are two ways to book a round of golf at Walton Heath Golf Club:

Phone:
+44 (0) 1737 812060

Email:
reception@waltonheath.com

HISTORY

Sir Henry Cosmo Bonsor was a deeply impressive man with a powerful résumé to match. In addition to his day-to-day duties, running the family brewery business, he was Conservative MP for Wimbledon, Chairman of London's Income Tax commission and a director of the Bank of England.

Sir Henry, as one of the original founders of Walton Heath Golf Club in 1903, assigned himself the task of commissioning an architect capable of turning the huge wilderness of rugged heathland he had recently

---

Price Guide: ● up to £49 | ● £50 – £99 | ● £100 – £149 | ● £150 – £200 | ● over £200

purchased, for the princely sum of £5,500, into a golf course that would stand the test of time.

Rather than seek the services of an established designer, Sir Henry opted to keep things in the family by appointing his brother-in-law who, by his own admission, was more of a 'huntin', shootin', cricketin' man', and had no previous experience whatsoever in course architecture.

Sir Henry's nepotistic opportunism would prove to be a masterstroke. His brother-in-law was Herbert Fowler.

Fowler's twin designs at Walton Heath – the Old course opened in 1904 followed by the New course in 1907 (originally as 9 holes and extended to 18 in 1913) – are regarded as the crown jewels within a portfolio considered among the very best.

As Fowler's journey toward golfing nobility began with his efforts at Walton Heath, the club itself has also enjoyed an enviable association with aristocracy. It is the only golf club in England to hold the distinction of having a reigning monarch as its (first) club captain. HRH The Prince of Wales

Evening shadows creep along the 2nd fairway on the Old Course. *Walton Heath Golf Club*

was already captain in 1936 when his father, George V, passed away, briefly becoming Edward VIII (although abdicating before his official coronation).

In addition to His Majesty, a host of sitting UK prime ministers regularly frequented Walton Heath. David Lloyd George, Andrew Bonar Law, Arthur Balfour and Winston Churchill are all counted as former members. It has often been said that at one time, as much government business was conducted in the clubhouse and on the fairways of Walton Heath as in the Palace of Westminster.

Other notable golfing royalty forever entwined with Walton Heath include James Braid, who became the club's first professional in 1904, playing in the inaugural match just a few days after his appointment. The five-time Open champion's association with the club would last until his death in 1950.

Braid's former workshop still resides behind the current pro shop and is now an eternal monument where visitors can pay homage to the great man as they make their way to the first tee.

In 1980, Walton Heath held a committee meeting with one item listed under 'any other business' – a request from the PGA to consider whether the club would like to host the Ryder Cup the following year.

This request prompted just one question, 'Could the course be ready in time?' The club secretary, Bill McCrea, responded with typical gusto – 'The course is always ready!'

Unfortunately for the newly formed Europe team, their opponents were also ready. One of the finest US teams ever amassed – with thirty-six major championships between them – would win the 1981 Ryder Cup easily 18½ – 9½.

PLAYING THE COURSE

Bernard Darwin, as he so often did, managed to perfectly articulate how it feels to play a round of golf in this

Old Course

General course information –

Par: 72 (Purple / White / Green) / 74 (Red)

S.S.S: 76 (Purple) / 73 (White) / 71 (Green) / 74 (Red)

Slope rating: 135 (Purple) / 131 (White) / 126 (Green) / 135 (Red)

Length: 5,937yds–7,331yds

Longest hole: Par-5 8th, 588yds (Purple) / Par-5 13th 512yds–497yds (White/Green) / Par-5 14th, 469yds (Red)

Shortest hole: Par-3 7th, 174yds–190yds (White/Purple) / Par-3 17th, 155yds (Green) / Par-3 11th, 132yds (Red)

Type: Heathland

charming corner of the Surrey sandbelt – 'if there is anything that golfers want and do not get at Walton Heath I do not know what it can be'.

It's a fair assumption most golfers want to find out how good they really are by testing themselves on a layout that has challenged the very best. To follow the same path as the greats of the game – Braid, Nicklaus, Trevino and Rose. To be inspired by their surroundings and feel a sense of awe at the tales it can tell. Walton Heath gives you all of this. What more could you possibly want?

The Old Course is generally regarded as the sterner test of the two layouts and offers a rather quirky opening as you play the 1st hole in isolation from the rest of the course. Originally a short par-4, it now plays as a long but fairly straight par-3.

Whichever tee you play from (all are available), it's a tricky carry to the putting surface. You can play a shot to the front and run onto the green, if you'd prefer, but you need to navigate past bunkers sat at the front on either side. From here, it's a short walk across Dorking Road to the remaining seventeen holes.

Seasoned members will tell you the ultimate 18-hole combination at Walton Heath would be the front-9 of the Old, followed by the back-9 of the New, where low scoring is typically at a premium. Holes 2 through to 6 on the Old are all par-4s (the 2nd and 4th are both par-5 from the red tees) of varying length with fairways flanked by heather and clever bunker positioning.

The 4th is the toughest hole on the course; despite the wide fairway a bunker is strategically located right in the centre, waiting to catch anything too long and straight. The 5th is a glorious par-4 with a narrow fairway that demands nothing less than a straight drive to steer clear of penal rough. Your approach needs to land short of the flag for an easier putt.

The front-9 closes with a dogleg left par-4, which needs a solid drive as far down the fairway as you can reach. Your approach needs to aim for the left side of the green to leave a better chance with your putter.

While the back-9 offers more low-scoring opportunities, the par-3 11th is another daunting tee-shot toward a green surrounded by bunkers. Anything short and left of the hole gives the best chance of your par or better.

The par-4 15th vies with the 4th as the toughest hole of the round. Your tee-shot needs to be either straight or slightly left to avoid heather and a trio of fairway bunkers along the right. Any approach shot hit too long on to the green could roll off the back, anything just short of the hole leaves an easier uphill putt.

16 **SIGNATURE HOLE: PAR-5 16TH, 433YDS–535YDS.**
A challenging finishing stretch continues with this real gem of a par-5.
Long hitters can definitely have a go at the green with the second
shot but first the drive must land right in the centre of the fairway.
Any short approach shots will likely head towards the greenside
bunker. If in doubt, leave yourself a pitch toward the left side of the
green.

Old Course holes and New Course holes in perfect harmony stretching across Walton Heath.
kevinmurraygolfphotography.com

The 17th is the last par-3 and needs a confident tee-shot toward the centre of the putting surface – be careful not to go too long as the back of the green is much narrower than the front.

The 18th is a worthy closing hole, tempting you to hit as close to the cross fairway bunker as you can get. Your approach needs to aim right at the pin on a long and undulating green for the best chance to finish with a good score.

New Course

General course information –

Par: 72 (Purple/White/Green) / 74 (Red)

S.S.S: 75 (Purple) / 72 (White) / 70 (Green) / 74 (Red)

Slope rating: 131 (Purple) / 125 (White) / 119 (Green) / 132 (Red)

Length: 5,907yds–7,199yds

Longest hole: Par-5 16th, 477yds–591yds

Shortest hole: Par-3 2nd 107yds–147yds

Type: Heathland

PLAYING THE COURSE

If you've come to Walton Heath looking for the most authentic experience of an original Herbert Fowler design, then it's the New Course you seek rather than the Old, remaining largely untouched since it was first open for play over a century ago.

An intriguing aspect of golf at Walton Heath, despite how, upon first sight, the layouts may appear 'as one', the Old and the New present a very different examination of your game.

Both courses tease you by leaving an opportunity to go through a gap between a variety of fairway obstacles to the green. Whereas the Old course favours a 'chip and run' approach, the New, awash with cross rough and strategic bunker locations, demands a solid 'pitch and stop'.

When you reach the first tee it's worth taking a few moments to appreciate the vast, wide open, expanse of 'the Heath' stretched out in front of you. Some of the world's finest heathland courses reside within a forty-mile radius of this neighbourhood, but none offer a vista quite like this.

The graceful criss-crossing of both courses is an unexpected delight and adds an intriguing dimension to your round as the layouts tease you into keeping one eye on which direction you will head from one hole to the next.

The New course is often adjudged as more forgiving than its older sibling, offering a slightly gentler experience for a wider spectrum of players. That's certainly the case with the 1st, 2nd and 4th holes, all of which offer you an early chance to feel very good about your game.

The 1st is a short par-4 with a slight dogleg left fairway. Longer hitters can look at taking a line for their drive to the right of the oak tree just off the left of the fairway. Shorter hitters should aim more to the right to leave a straightforward approach toward a large, flat green.

The short par-3 at the 2nd (the shortest hole on the course) is all about the tee-shot – get that right and you're on for a good score. The long par-4 3rd may check your momentum before you reach the driveable par-4 4th.

This is a clear risk/reward hole goading you to go for the green, but beware the bunkers front left and right waiting for anything off target. Just as many birdies or pars are made here by leaving a gentle pitch from the left side of the fairway.

Blue sky above the heath on the New Course. *Walton Heath Golf Club*

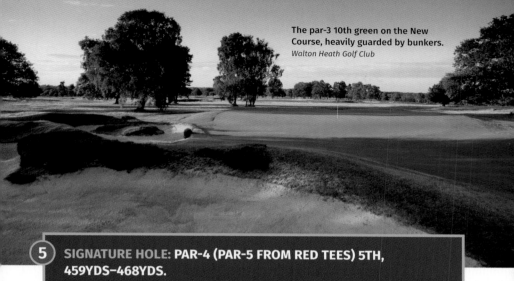

The par-3 10th green on the New Course, heavily guarded by bunkers.
Walton Heath Golf Club

(5) SIGNATURE HOLE: PAR-4 (PAR-5 FROM RED TEES) 5TH, 459YDS–468YDS.

It's possible your experience up to this point has left you dreaming of scorecards sent from heaven and feeling like Tiger or Rory. Beware, this is the hole where the New Course rings its bell to tell you playtime's over and begins to show its teeth.

All the trouble from the tee is on the right side of the fairway with thick heather and two bunkers eager for some catching practice. The fairway slopes to the left and this side gives you the best angle for your approach into the green protected by two bunkers at the front.

The par-5 8th offers plenty of leeway off the tee with a wide fairway. The second shot must navigate over a range of cross-fairway mounds, avoiding a trio of bunkers to leave an approach that should aim toward the back of the green and missing a sharp slope at the front.

The back-9 starts with the final par-3 at the 10th. All the trouble here is at the front with three bunkers left and right. Go with an extra club if in doubt. The par-4 12th and par-5 13th were selected from the new course as part of the composite 18 holes for the 2018 British Master's tournament and it's easy to see why. Many a promising scorecard has hit the wall here.

Your tee-shot at the 12th is slightly unsighted and leaves the impression you have less fairway to land your ball on than is actually the case. Hit towards the centre of the green in the distance for the perfect line.

The 13th is a fairly straight hole, but slightly uphill. A large fairway bunker on the right is in play for the longer hitters at 300yds from the back tees. The green here slopes back to front, therefore putting from the front of the green is the best option.

The 18th on the New was used as the closing hole for the 1981 Ryder Cup. This is where Dave Marr's incredible team stood to make their final swings as they stormed to victory.

Between the tee-box and the main fairway is a deep valley leaving no margin for error. Your tee shot should aim to get as close to the large fairway bunker protecting the green. Anything down the middle will leave you with an approach pitch towards an unsighted putting surface.

Other courses in the area

The Surrey/Berkshire sandbelt is home to some of the world's finest heathland courses. Below is a further wonderful selection, all within easy driving distance of those mentioned in this section.

● **HANKLEY COMMON GOLF CLUB**
Opened in 1897 as a 9-hole course until James Braid extended it by a further nine in 1922. Harry Colt then redesigned the layout in 1936. The course sits within a site of special scientific interest on a large expanse of land and has a very open feel to it. Often described as one of the finest examples of a hybrid links/heathland course in the UK.

Website: www.hankley.co.uk
Email: proshop@hankley.co.uk
Telephone: +44 (0) 1252 792493

Par: 71 / 72 (Red)
Length: 5,572yds–6,909yds
Type: Heathland

Fees:
● per round (weekdays)
● per round (weekends)
● County card

The three 'W's'

● **WORPLESDON GOLF CLUB**
Founded in 1908. The course creation was a joint effort between John Abercromby and

Willie Park Jr. The club's most famous association was with Joyce Wethered, one of the finest golfers of her generation.

Visitors are welcome on weekdays. Handicap certificates are required (maximum 20 for men and 30 for ladies).

Website: www.worplesdongc.co.uk
Email: office@worplesdongc.co.uk
Telephone: +44 (0) 1483 472277

Par: 71 (White/Yellow) / 73 (Red)
Length: 5,660yds–6,466yds
Type: Heathland

Fees:
(Low season)
● per round

(High season)
● per round

● WOKING GOLF CLUB
Revered golf writer (and former club president), Bernard Darwin described Woking as "The best and pleasantest place to play golf I have ever known."

Visitors are welcome on weekdays (except Bank Holidays). Handicap certificates are required (maximum 24 for men and 30 for ladies). Play is usually a 2-ball format with singles in the morning and foursomes in the afternoon.

Website: www.wokinggolfclub.co.uk
Email: info@wokinggolfclub.co.uk
Telephone: +44 (0) 1483 760053

Par: 70 (Black/White/Yellow) / 73 (Red)
Length: 5,710yds–6,606yds

Type: Heathland

Fees:
(Low season)
● per round

(High season)
● per round
● per day
● twilight rate

● WEST HILL GOLF CLUB
Founded in 1907. A real heathland gem that has remained largely unaltered since its creation by Cuthbert Butchart, the club's first professional. Surrounded by large pines, West Hill is renowned for having one of the most challenging array of par-3 holes in the UK.

Website: www.westhillgc.co.uk
Email: secretary@westhill-golfclub.co.uk
Telephone: +44 (0) 1483 474365

Par: 69 (White/Yellow) / 74 (Red)
Length: 5,643yds–6,457yds
Type: Heathland

Fees:
(Low season)
● per round

(High season)
● per round / day rate
● twilight rate

Kent Coast

PRINCE'S GOLF CLUB

Sandwich Bay,
Sandwich,
Kent, CT13 9QB
www.princesgolfclub.co.uk
Phone: + 44 (0) 1304 611118
Email: office@princesgolfclub.co.uk

Handicap Certificate: not required

Green fees:
(Low season)
● per round (18 holes)

(Shoulder season)
● per round (18 holes)

(High season)
● per round (18 holes – Mon to Thurs)
● per round (18 holes – Fri to Sun)

'Links and Lodges' golf breaks: *
(Low season)
● Midweek & weekend

(Shoulder season)
● Midweek
● Weekend

(High season)
● Midweek & weekend

(* = includes one night lodge
accommodation (on site), two
rounds of golf, à la carte breakfast.

Shoulder and low season packages
also include two-course dinner.)

Caddies:
£60 per round. Paid in cash +
gratuity. To book in advance ring
the caddiemaster based at Royal
St George's, +44 (0) 1304 613090

Equipment hire:
Clubs, buggies and trolleys are
available for hire from the pro shop,
+44 (0) 1304 695569

How do I book a round of golf?
Prince's welcomes visitors at
all times during the week and
throughout the year to play
the Shore, Dunes and Himalayas
courses.

There are three ways to book a
round of golf at Prince's Golf Club:

Online:
www.princesgolfclub.co.uk

Phone:
+44 (0) 1304 611118

Email:
office@princesgolfclub.co.uk

Price Guide: ● up to £49 | ● £50 – £99 | ● £100 – £149 | ● £150 – £200 | ● over £200

HISTORY

Percy Belgrave 'Laddie' Lucas was born in the old clubhouse at Prince's in 1915 and spent his formative years learning to play golf on the links course. Following the outbreak of the Second World War, he became a pilot in the RAF. During a dogfight over the English Channel, a hit from an enemy Messerschmitt crippled Laddie's spitfire.

Maintaining control just long enough to reach Sandwich Bay before the engine failed, rather than bale out, he was able to glide his plane towards the familiar site of Prince's clubhouse and executed a perfect landing alongside the original 9th-hole fairway (a commemorative spitfire propeller raised on a wooden post marks the exact landing site next to what is now the 3rd hole of the Himalayas course).

Known affectionately as Prince's 'favourite son' by members past and present, Laddie Lucas could well be the only golfer in the history of the game whose association with their home course can genuinely be described as life saving.

Good scores can be made on the Dunes par-5 6th hole if you can thread your way past the fairway bunkers. *Jason Livy Photography*

The Lucas family's connection with Prince's Golf Club dates back to its formation in 1906. Laddie's father, Percy Montagu Lucas, was a close friend of the club's founder, Sir Harry Mallaby-Deeley, and became the first secretary. Arthur J. Balfour, fresh from his stint as UK prime minister, was appointed the first club captain.

The original 18-hole links course was a joint creation between Percy M. and the 1902 amateur champion, Charles Hutchings. At just under 7,000yds, the new layout was designed with an eye on countering the impact of the new Haskell ball and was greeted with much enthusiasm by the local golfing community.

After surviving the First World War relatively unscathed, the club and it's course would thrive during the 1920s and 30s, undoubtedly reaching the pinnacle in 1932 when it hosted the Open Championship for the first (and, to date only) time. Gene Sarazon would emerge victorious, leading through all four rounds, at the same time introducing his new club – the sand wedge – to the golfing public.

The Second World War would bring an end to this golden era for Prince's. Commandeered by the military for battle training, the original course was almost entirely destroyed. The land was eventually decommissioned in 1949 and a year later Sir Guy Campbell and John Morrison were appointed to design a new layout.

Fortunately, the architects were able to incorporate seventeen of the original greens within a new 27-hole championship links. This unique layout, spread across three looping 9-hole courses – Shore, Dunes and Himalayas – all starting and ending beside the clubhouse, is the one that greets you today.

PLAYING THE COURSE

Sir Harry Mallaby-Deeley's original vision for Prince's was as a club always willing to extend the hand of friendship to each and every golfer – young and old, male and female.

Dunes

General course information –

Par: 36 / 38 (Red)

S.S.S: 37 (Blue) / 36 (White) / 35 (Yellow) / 36 (Red)

Slope rating: 130 (Blue) / 123 (White) / 118 (Yellow) / 123 (Red)

Length: 2,787yds-3,634yds

Longest hole: Par-5 3rd, 484yds-569yds (Red tees - par-5 6th, 415yds)

Shortest hole: Par-3 2nd, 140yds-170yds

Type: Links

Before you venture out onto the links and commence battle against the cold, icy winds blowing in from across the channel you're assured the warmest of welcomes from everyone in the clubhouse. Whatever your score, just relax and remember – you're among friends here.

With three 9-hole layouts to choose from, what you're also guaranteed to receive at Prince's is a vintage 'links and a half' golf experience unlike any other in the UK. If you opt to start your round at the Dunes course, be sure to have left time for a few practise swings in advance as the opening hole makes no apology for throwing you in at the deep end.

1 **SIGNATURE HOLE: PAR-4 1ST, 404YDS–433YDS.**
Regarded as one of the toughest holes on the entire complex. A sharp dogleg right to left, (long) par-4 generally played into the prevailing wind towards a narrow 'hogsback' green.

Aim to the left of the bunker in the centre of the fairway from the tee for the best line in for your approach. With drop offs on either side, the green is not easy to hit. Any score on or near par here is a very good start.

The challenging opening continues with a tricky par-3 that tends to need one more club than you're thinking, particularly if the wind's blowing. Best to aim left of the green as anything too far right may roll towards a large bunker on this side.

Hole 3 is a fairly short par-5, achievable in two for longer hitters, offering an opportunity to claw back any dropped shots against your handicap up to now. Keep right off the tee to avoid the fairway bunkers but not too far as a brook runs along this side of the fairway.

After two more testing par-4s at holes four and five, the 6th is another par-5 that rewards straight, accurate golf shots. Try and avoid all the fairway bunkers as you plot your way towards one of the longest greens on the course. Set atop a large sand dune with a steep drop off on the left and a ditch waiting for any errant approach shots.

The 8th is a long par-3 (217yds from the back tees) with a large bunker protecting the left side of the green so best to keep right with your tee-shot. There's room at the front of the putting surface for anything dropping short but any chip landing on the left could feed down into the bunker.

Himalayas

General course information –

Par: 36

S.S.S: 38 (Blue) / 36 (White) / 35 (Yellow) / 37 (Red)

Slope rating: 140 (Blue) / 131 (White) / 128 (Yellow) / 133 (Red)

Length: 2,818yds-3,611yds

Longest hole: Par-5 2nd, 500yds-620yds

Shortest hole: Par-3 5th, 103yds-143yds

Type: Links

PLAYING THE COURSE

Even before the extensive remodelling work – undertaken by revered course architects Mackenzie & Ebert – was completed in 2018 the Himalayas course was a firm favourite among members and regular visitors looking for a fun, quick-fire 9-holes.

This view was often seen as, perhaps, a sentimental one and akin to the old adage of rooting for the underdog. However, these renovations have resulted in a significant change in Prince's traditional 'pecking order' with Himalayas now, arguably, the most striking section of the 27-hole layout.

The sun sets over Sandwich Bay and the splendidly named 'Bloody Point', par-3 5th hole on the Himalayas course. *Jason Livy Photography*

Prince's has always been a club able to extend a hearty welcome. The reinvented Himalayas course is now testament to its willingness to listen to feedback from the golfing fraternity. They wanted driveable par-4s, challenging par-5s and picturesque par-3s. And now they've got them.

In direct contrast to the opening hole on the Dunes course, Himalayas provides a more gentle start. The 1st is a mid-length par-4 offering a fairly wide fairway with lots of space to aim for off the tee. Any approach shot needs to avoid out of bounds along the left and a sleepered bunker on the right towards a small green.

From hereon in the Himalayas begins to show its teeth. On the site of the original 2nd and 3rd holes now sits a formidable par-5 (622yds from the back tees). The lone fir tree standing on the right of the fairway is your marker from the tee. Your second shot should keep right to avoid bunkers positioned on the left. Any approach needs to take account of a green which slopes back to front.

On your way to the 3rd tee you're greeted by the unusual sight of a spitfire propeller, placed here to commemorate the site of Laddie Lucas' landing during the Second World War. This hole requires accurate golf shots all the way to a large, shared green (with the eighth hole).

(5) SIGNATURE HOLE: PAR-3 5TH, 103YDS-143YDS, 'BLOODY POINT'.
The newest addition to the Himalayas following its reconstruction and the shortest hole on the entire course, named after the fearsome Battle of Sandwich between the West Saxons and the Vikings in AD 851.

This is the only hole that plays directly towards the shoreline. Any seasoned links golfer knows never to be fooled by such short yardage. Your club choice will be dictated by the strength (and direction) of the wind. Steep run-offs on all sides make the green a treacherous one to hang on to. Any par here should be savoured.

The 8th is a classic risk/reward par-4 tempting you to have a blast towards the green. While the reward is clear, so is the risk with water hazards, deep bunkers and large run-off areas waiting for any misjudged tee-shots.

The 9th is a testing finishing hole. Aim between the fairway bunkers, left and right, for the best line into the green. Your approach needs to avoid the fabled 'Sarazen bunker' sitting near to the left of the putting surface. If you land in the sand, at the very least you get to pay your respects to the man who introduced to the world the club you'll need to get out.

Shore

General course information –

Par: 36 / 38 (Red)

S.S.S: 37 (Blue) / 36 (White) / 35 (Yellow) / 37 (Red)

Slope rating: 125 (Blue) / 118 (White) / 113 (Yellow) / 125 (Red)

Length: 2,759yds-3,643yds

Longest hole: Par-5 8th, 512yds-568yds

Shortest hole: Par-3 5th, 103yds-158yds

Type: Links

PLAYING THE COURSE

The Shore traditionally plays as the inward-9 of the 18-hole combination used during regional qualifying for The Open Championship (Dunes/ Shore). As the name suggests this layout provides the 'smell' of the sea one would most associate with a links course, looping in a clockwise direction out towards the far perimeter of the property and running alongside Prince's royal neighbour.

The 1st hole is a tough opener. Your tee-shot needs to steer clear of two fairway bunkers along the right but try to not stray too far left as a pot bunker is also in play along this side. Your approach needs to avoid aiming too far left as the elevated green slopes away steeply leaving a tricky chip back on to the putting surface.

The 3rd is the first of two par-3s on the Shore-9 and requires an accurate tee-shot to achieve a par-score. Anything left could find a deep pot bunker waiting at the front of the green, anything right will leave a blind chip shot onto the putting surface.

---

5 SIGNATURE HOLE: PAR-3 5TH, 103YDS-158YDS, 'SMUGGLERS LANDING'.

After a testing par-4 at the 4th you reach the newest member of Prince's fine par-3 collection. And what an addition. Visually stunning, with the backdrop of the shoreline and the white cliffs of Ramsgate in the far distance. The hole name derives from the smuggling trade so prevalent along the Kent coast in the 1700s and a particular incident between two rival gangs in 1746.

Surrounded by sand dunes between the tee-box and the redan style green. Nothing less than straight at the putting surface will do to secure your par at this modern classic built in homage to a golden era.

**Aerial view of the newest addition to Prince's par-3 collection, the 5th hole on the Shore Course -
Smugglers Landing.** *Jason Livy Photography*

The 6th and 7th holes are both challenging par-4s requiring accurate drives
to stand any chance of a par. The Shore-9's long holes all have a variety of
strategically placed fairway bunkers, which all appear to be in play and the
7th is no different. If you manage to navigate past the three sand hazards
your approach shot needs to aim left for the best chance of staying on the
green. Don't be too downhearted with a bogey score here.

The closing hole is a long par-4 with an unforgiving fairway. Use the far
flagpole beside the clubhouse in the distance for the best line from the tee.
Any uneven bounce too far left or right could see your ball spring into the
rough. The ground is relatively flat around the putting surface so any final
approach can afford to run up towards the green.

(28)

THE ROYAL ST GEORGE'S GOLF CLUB

Sandwich,
Kent,
CT13 9PB
www.royalstgeorges.com
Phone: +44 (0) 1304 613090
Email: office@royalstgeorges.com

General course information –
Par: 70 (Championship / Medal /
Weekday) / 74 (Pinto)

S.S.S: 75 – Championship / 72(Men's),
79(Ladies) – Medal / 71(M), 77(L) -
Weekday / 68(M), 75(L) – Pinto

Slope rating: 138 (Championship) /
133(Men), 146(Ladies) – Medal / 129(M),
140(L) – Weekday / 115(M), 134(L) - Pinto

Length: 5,801yds–7,204yds

Longest hole: Par-5 14th, 487yds–
533yds (Par-5 7th, 573yds – Champ tees)

Shortest hole: Par-3 6th, 140yds–152yds
(Par-3 16th, 161yds – Champ tees)

Type: Links

Typically, visitors will play from the
tee of the day, however, all tees are
available (including championship)
at all times should you wish to use
them.

Handicap Certificate: Required
(maximum handicap is 18 for both
men and ladies).

Green fees:
(Low season)
● per round

(Shoulder season)
● per round

(High season)
● per round

Caddies:
£50.00 per round. Caddie fees
to be paid in cash (+ gratuity).
Highly recommended and, in some
circumstances, mandatory at the
discretion of the club.

Equipment hire:
Clubs, buggies (with medical
certificate), electric trolleys and pull
trolleys can be hired from the pro shop.

How do I book a round of golf?
Royal St George's welcomes visitors
at the following times during the
week:

Monday	9.30 am – 12.30 pm and 2.30 pm onwards (2 ball)
Tuesday	8.30 pm – 11.30 am and 1.30 pm – 3.30 pm (3 or 4 ball)

Price Guide: ● up to £49 | ● £50 – £99 | ● £100 – £149 | ● £150 – £200 | ● over £200

Wednesday–		**Online:**
Friday	9.30 am – 12.30 pm	www.royalstgeorges.com/Online
	and 2.30 pm onwards	Booking
	(2 ball)	

Online:
www.royalstgeorges.com/Online Booking

Weekends and Bank Holidays are reserved for members and their guests.

Phone:
+44 (0) 1304 613090

Email:
office@royalstgeorges.com

There are three ways to book a round of golf at Royal St George's Golf Club:

HISTORY

Dr William Laidlaw Purves, a prominent ophthalmic surgeon from Edinburgh, made it his mission to bring the delights of Scottish links golf to the south coast of England, while working at Guy's Hospital in London. Purves was already a notable figure in golfing circles having played a major role in the creation of the Ladies Golf Union and involvement in the formulation of the handicap rules.

After a long and laboured search, in 1886 Dr Purves and his friends spotted a patch of land, while stood atop the St Clement's Church tower in Sandwich, they all agreed would be perfect for a links course. One year later, St George's Golf Club was formed, receiving its Royal patronage in 1902 from Edward VII. The Prince of Wales and future King of England – Edward VIII – also served as club captain from 1927–28.

In 1894, just seven years after its formation, Royal St George's began its long association with The Open Championship, becoming the first English host venue of the tournament. In all, the club has hosted The Open fourteen times – the most for any English venue and fourth overall behind only Muirfield, Prestwick and St Andrews. This figure will rise to fifteen following the 149th edition, due to be held in 2021.

In addition to The Open, Royal St George's has also hosted the Amateur Championship thirteen times, the British PGA Championship five times, the Walker Cup on two occasions and the Curtis Cup in 1988.

Notable historical members include the author Ian Fleming, creator of the most famous spy in movie history – James Bond, 007. Royal St George's provided the course layout for Royal St Marks, described in Fleming's Bond novel, *Goldfinger*.

The view that greets you from the 1st tee at Royal St. George's. *Jason Livy Photography*

As their round is about to start, Goldfinger uses the practice putting green while Bond walks straight to the first tee. Canny old members have often chuckled at this subtle homage by Fleming, as the speed of the practice green historically bears no resemblance to those out on the course at Royal St George's. Bond, of course, goes on to win the match.

Fleming, who played to a handicap of 9 (the same as his secret service agent alter-ego), rarely changed the names of locations in his novels but made an exception in this case, as it is said he wanted to avoid an increase in membership at his beloved golf club as a result of the book's popularity.

PLAYING THE COURSE

Standing on the banks of the English Channel, the course at Royal St George's resides in splendid seclusion, protected from the hustle and bustle of everyday life. This is why the world's greatest spy novelist loved it so much.

Other than the removal of the blind-tee shots at both the 3rd and 8th holes and a re-routing of the 11th, the layout has remained true to the original design. Rather than adopt the traditional '9-out, 9-back', the course follows more of a loop with no two holes playing in the same direction. As a result, the wind can often play a major factor here.

When the wind howls in off the sea, any attempt to lower your handicap may have to wait for the next round. However, on a still day even the most humble golfer can stride off the 18th green with an extra spring in their step.

The unpredictability of what your scorecard may throw up is not confined to the ordinary amateur. Throughout its Open history, Royal St George's is well known for its wild scoring spectrum. Jack Nicklaus, still in his pomp, took an 83 here in 1981 whereas Ernie Els, in 1993, became the first player to shoot all four rounds of The Open in the 60s. Unfortunately for the Big Easy, Greg Norman was following right behind him to claim the Claret Jug.

The fairways here have been described as 'having the topography of an unmade bed', with every hump, lump and bump ready to catapult your ball in an unexpected direction. If you do find the fairways, don't count on too many flat lies for your next shot. This is links golf at its erratic, uncompromising, best.

With the large bunker looming on the right, it's definitely best to aim left at the 4th tee.
Jason Livy Photography

The par-4 1st is no easy opener, requiring a 250yd carry from the back tees to clear 'the kitchen' valley running across the fairway. The green slopes away from you and is protected by three bunkers front-left. If you want to play safe aim for the gully along the right.

Hole 3 is the first par-3 and it's a long one. There are no bunkers here – the only non-bunker par-3 on The Open rota – but the two-tiered green more than makes up for this as any putt from the back down towards the hole requires a very steady hand.

The par-4 4th is one of the signature holes at Royal St George's and home to one of the largest fairway bunkers in the UK, which looms large as you line up your drive from the tee. The removal of the sleeper bunkers from around the edge makes it no less intimidating.

If you manage to navigate around the 'mountain' hazard, your approach into the green needs to be accurate to avoid falling into a valley at the front or, if you're long, out-of-bounds at the back. Pars are rare here.

(6) SIGNATURE HOLE: PAR-3 6TH, 140YDS–176YDS, 'THE MAIDEN'.
After the first sight of the shoreline at hole 5, this mid-length par-3 is named after the shape of the towering dunes surrounding it. If your tee-shot manages to safely navigate the dunes, there's also the small matter of four bunkers protecting a two-tiered green. Only straight at the centre will do.

Bunkers prowl the back of the 6th green, Maiden hole.
Jason Livy Photography

The back-9 starts with the notorious par-4 10th, which saw Tom Kite's hopes of becoming champion golfer of the year in 1985 disappear in the deep bunkers either side of the elevated green (he found both). Members will tell you that a long approach toward the back of the infinity green is preferred as it falls away sharply on all sides.

In *Goldfinger*, Ian Fleming described the 10th at Royal St Marks (aka Royal St George's) as the most dangerous hole on the course, where a misplaced second shot will 'break many hearts' – you've been warned.

The closing stretch of holes from 13 through to 18 is as tough as any on The Open rota. The long par-4 13th fairway has bunkers left, right and centre. Your approach shot has to be straight at the centre of the green. Anything short can be caught by two front bunkers, anything long could land over on the Prince's course directly behind.

After the hardest hole on the course (another long, punishing par-4 at the 15th), the green at the last par-3, 16th is ring-fenced with bunkers – one of which finally put paid to Thomas Bjorn's hopes of getting his hands on the Claret Jug in 2003. If you score a bogey here, take solace in the fact you're still one up on a winning Ryder Cup captain.

The round concludes with two more testing par-4s, none more so than the 18th. Your drive should aim left to leave the best line into the green for your approach and avoid the infamous 'Duncan's hollow' at the front left of the putting surface. Sandy Lyle landed here in 1985 but managed to cling on, dropping just one shot, before claiming his crown.

View from the 18th tee down the final fairway at Royal St. George's.
Jason Livy Photography

29

ROYAL CINQUE PORTS GOLF CLUB

Golf Road,
Deal,
Kent,
CT14 6RF
www.royalcinqueports.com
Phone: +44 (0) 1304 374007
Email: office@royalcinqueports.com

General course information –
Par: 72 (Black/White/Yellow/Blue) / 73 (Red)

S.S.S: 76 (Black) / 74 (White) / 72 (Yellow) / 67 (Blue) / 73 (Red)

Slope rating: 131 (Black) / 129 (White) / 125 (Yellow) / 112 (Blue) / 124 (Red)

Length: 5,660yds–7,367yds

Longest hole: Par-5 5th, 600yds (Black) / Par-5 3rd, 423yds–566yds (Red-White)

Shortest hole: Par-3 4th, 111yds–151yds

Type: Links

Handicap Certificate: Required (maximum handicap is 22 for men and 36 for ladies).

Green fees:
(Low season)
● per round / day rate (Weekdays & Weekend)

(Shoulder season)
● per round / day rate (Weekdays)
● per round/ day rate (Weekend)

(High season)
● per round / ● day rate (Weekdays & Weekend)

Twilight rate:
● after 3.30 pm

Caddies:
£40.00 per player (+ gratuity). Available upon request (must be booked in advance via pro shop, +44 (0) 1304 374170 / professional@ royalcinqueports.com)

Equipment hire:
Clubs, buggies and trolleys can be hired from the pro shop

How do I book a round of golf?
Royal Cinque Ports welcomes visitors at the following times during the week to play the championship links:

Monday & Thursday (from 8.30 am)	Fourballs
Tues/Wed/Sat/ Sun (afternoons only)	Foursomes/ 2-ball singles
Friday (Afternoons*)	Foursomes/ 2-ball singles

Price Guide: ● up to £49 | ● £50 – £99 | ● £100 – £149 | ● £150 – £200 | ● over £200

* = some availability in the mornings

There are three ways to book a round of golf at Royal Cinque Ports Golf Club:

Online:
www.royalcinqueports.com/Visitor Booking

Phone:
+44 (0) 1304 374007

Email:
office@royalcinqueports.com

HISTORY

Plans for a golf course in the seaside town of Deal had been mooted among a group of prominent gentlemen since 1890. It would not be until May 1892 before the first members began swinging their clubs around the original 9-hole course at Cinque Ports Golf Club.

Among those awarded club captaincy during its infancy was Arthur J. Balfour in 1898, around the same time as the course at Cinque Ports expanded from 9 to 18 holes. Four years later, Balfour would have to bring a halt to any notion of regular rounds of golf when he succeeded his Uncle, Lord Salisbury, as Prime Minister of Great Britain.

Aerial view of the 3rd and 4th greens at Royal Cinque Ports. *Jason Livy Photography*

Harry Hunter, who would go on to have a fifty-year association with the club as greenkeeper and club professional, designed the original 9-hole links layout. So impressed by the course some years earlier, James Braid took charge of a redesign following the Great War in 1919. Sir Guy Campbell and Henry Cotton combined their expertise to bring the course back to life in 1946 following the ravages of the Second World War.

Royal Cinque Ports has enjoyed a long and proud association with the monarchy stretching back to the turn of the twentieth century. King George V accepted patronage of the club, bestowing its royal title in 1910. Both he and his son, Edward VIII, were regular visitors to Deal. In 1949 the patronage was reconfirmed by George VI.

The club has hosted The Open Championship on two occasions in 1909 and 1920. However, Royal Cinque Ports has had some rotten luck with regards further hosting duties, losing out on the 1915 Open (postponed due to the war) and an abnormally high tide washing over the course causing both the 1938 and 1949 tournaments to be switched to nearby Royal St George's.

PLAYING THE COURSE

If your definition of a great round of golf is one full of character, excitement and a healthy dose of fun then look no further – it's here. The championship course at Royal Cinque Ports is a natural links masterpiece, providing every challenge in the book.

If any more persuasion were required to take a trip down to England's southeast coast, this is what a five-time Open Champion and member of the great triumvirate had to say about his experience here:

> After another opportunity of playing over the Deal course I am still of the opinion I previously expressed that it is the best course I have played in England.
>
> – James Braid, 1904.

Despite its glorious setting edged right up along the pebble-beached coastline, this is a course that can – and frequently has – punished the very best.

One of golf's finest, most flamboyant showmen, Walter 'The Haig' Hagen won two of his four Open Championships up the road at Royal St George's, but would leave Deal (as RCP is often referred) licking his wounds, finishing in second to last place following his first attempt at the claret jug in 1920.

This was a challenging course then, and it's a challenging course now.

A traditional 9-out and 9-back layout with the first hole playing across the front of the clubhouse. Conventional wisdom oft repeated among seasoned-members and many 'battled-scarred' visitors suggests all your chances of low scoring are to be found on the first eleven holes, played with the wind behind you, before clinging on to your hats for the final seven holes – reputedly the hardest 7-hole closing stretch in the UK. Calm days can be rare in this part of the world.

The first three opening holes remain almost completely true to their original design – same greens but with longer fairways. Hole 1 is a fairly gentle opener, but watch for the burn at the front of the green – better to be long than short with your approach.

The 3rd hole is the first par-5 with a clear risk/reward dilemma off the tee. Aiming as close as you can to the fairway bunkers on the right, without going in them, will give you the best line toward the green. Long hitters may be able to reach the green in two, which sits down in a large hollow. This hole looks beautiful but can happily play ugly.

From the first par-5 onto the first par-3 at the 4th. No bunkers at this hole, but your tee-shot needs to be accurate to stay on the upturned saucer green. The remaining front-9 holes continue along the coastline.

The 6th is a tremendous, short, dogleg-right par-4 and the signature hole on the outward stretch, presenting another risk/reward conundrum tempting

The 6th green sits high above the undulating fairway. Any approach shot pushed too long could find the beach directly behind. *Jason Livy Photography*

the big hitters to go for the green. Get it right and you're on for a good score, get it too far right and you're on the beach.

Hole 8 is a testing par-3 with the front of the green surrounded by six bunkers. Anything from a wedge or a hybrid may be needed depending on how strong the wind is blowing. Anything high and straight at the centre will be fine.

The inward-9 begins with a par-4 at the 10th, described as one of the finest two-shot holes in England. Long hitters can get close from the tee, but whether short or long, the best approach needs to drop short and run onto an uphill green avoiding the bunker front-right.

The 12th hole is where the tough inward stretch begins and you feel the fierce wind turn against you. Every shot you make from here needs to be as accurate as can be. Aim left from the tee to give yourself the best line into the green with your approach aimed right toward the green avoiding a pot bunker sitting front-left.

(16) SIGNATURE HOLE: PAR-5 16TH, 416YDS–549YDS.

Of all the terrific holes on this course, the 16th at Royal Cinque Ports is the one that will stay with you long after your round has come to an end.

Take a big gulp and an even bigger swing to make sure your drive reaches the start of the fairway. Aim for the only bunker you can see from the tee as your guide. The good news is, the recent re-introduction of a previously lost fairway on the left-hand side now gives you more options for your approach towards a small, elevated green. Any net-par score at this hole should be one to treasure.

Aerial view of the 16th green at Royal Cinque Ports.
Jason Livy Photography

Two more tricky par-4s remain at 17 and 18 to bring you back to the clubhouse. From the 18th tee aim just left of the clubhouse flag in the distance for the perfect line onto a wide fairway. Take one more club than you think for your approach to clear the ditch running across the fairway towards a raised green.

18-hole courses nearby

● LITTLESTONE GOLF CLUB

Just under an hour's drive along the coast from Royal Cinque Ports, Littlestone's championship course is considered a real hidden gem. Primarily a two-ball course (Tuesdays & Thursdays), three and four balls are also welcome at certain times during the week.

Website: www.littlestonegolfclub.org.uk
Email: info@littlestonegolfclub.org.uk
Phone: +44 (0) 1797 363355

Par: 71 / 73 (Red)
Length: 5,717yds–6,632yds
Type: Links

Fees:
● per round

In addition to the championship course, Littlestone has a smaller 18-hole course called The Warren also available for visitors to play:

Par: 67 / 69 (Red)
Length: 4,847yds–5,241yds
Type: Links

Fees:
● per round

● WALMER AND KINGSDOWN GOLF CLUB

Perched on top of the white cliffs of Dover, every hole offers a sea view and on a clear day you can see all the way across the channel to France. Originally designed by James Braid and just a five-mile drive down the coast from Royal Cinque Ports.

Website: www.kingsdowngolf.co.uk
Email: info@kingsdowngolf.co.uk
Phone: +44 (0) 1304 373256

Par: 72 / 74 (Red)
Length: 5,842yds–6,471yds
Type: Downland

Fees:
● per round

SOUTH WEST

BURNHAM & BERROW GOLF CLUB – THE CHAMPIONSHIP COURSE

St Christopher's Way,
Burnham-on-Sea,
Somerset,
TA8 2PE
www.burnhamandberrowgolfclub.co.uk
Phone: +44 (0) 1278 785760
Email: office@
burnhamandberrowgolfclub.co.uk

General course information –
Par: 71 (Green/White/Yellow) / 74 (Red)

S.S.S: 75 (Green) / 74 (White) / 72 (Yellow) / 74 (Red)

Slope rating: 132 (Green) / 127 (White) / 124 (Yellow) / 127 (Red)

Length: 5,768yds–7,001yds

Longest hole: Par-5 13th, 476yds–566yds

Shortest hole: Par-3 9th, 182yds (Green) / Par-3 5th, 147yds–160yds (White/Yellow) / Par-3 14th 120yds (Red)

Type: Links

Handicap Certificate: Required (maximum 22 for men and 30 for ladies)

Green fees:
(Low season)
● per round
● 27 holes*

(High season)
● per round
● 27 holes*

* = one round on the Championship course and one round on the Channel course

Caddies:
£50.00 (+ gratuity). Must be booked in advance via the pro shop
+44 (0) 1278 785760

Equipment hire:
Buggies, trolleys and clubs all available for hire from the pro shop. Recommended to book buggies in advance, if required.

How do I book a round of golf?
Burnham and Berrow welcomes visitors after 11 am from Sunday to Friday (Saturday tee-times are reserved for members and their guests).

There are three ways to book a round of golf at Burnham and Berrow Golf Club:

Price Guide: ● up to £49 | ● £50 – £99 | ● £100 – £149 | ● £150 – £200 | ● over £200

Online:
www.burnhamandberrowgolfclub.
co.uk/Visitors tee bookings

Email:
office@burnhamandberrowgolfclub.
co.uk

Phone:
+44 (0) 1278 785760

HISTORY

Sport is blessed with countless tales of siblings reaching the summit of their respective discipline – Venus & Serena Williams, Jack & Bobby Charlton, Peyton & Eli Manning. But have you ever heard the story about three brothers who played in the same Ryder Cup?

Ernest, Charles and Reg Whitcombe, all prominent professional golfers during the 1920s and '30s, were selected to represent Great Britain against the US in the 1935 tournament held at Ridgewood Country Club, New Jersey. Charles, captaining the GB side for the second time (and would be chosen for this role again in 1937 and 1949), was regarded as the most talented golfer of the three, despite younger brother Reg securing the only major title for the Whitcombe family when he became Champion Golfer of the Year in 1938.

Despite their best efforts, the GB team were beaten 9 – 3 by a dominant US team, which included the likes of Walter Hagen and Gene Sarazen.

The Whitcombes were born and raised in a small cottage next to St Mary's Church in the seaside village of Berrow, overlooking the championship course at Burnham and Berrow Golf Club. It was here that Ernest, Charles and Reg developed their love for the game.

Following a meeting held among twelve local gentlemen at the Royal Clarence Hotel, the club was officially established in 1890, initially playing their golf on a 9-hole course designed by Royal North Devon's club pro, Charles Gibson. Over the next thirty years, the course would undergo a series of redesigns by some of the finest architects of their time (or any time, for that matter).

By 1897, Gibson had added a further nine holes to the layout. In 1910, Herbert Fowler and his assistant, Hugh Alison (both members of the club), extended the layout to over 6,000yds and were the creators of the famous Church hole (12th).

In 1913 Harry Colt produced a new blueprint which is, in essence, the layout that remains to this day, stripping away all of the blind shots and replacing

Long evening shadows begin to creep over the championship course at Burnham & Berrow.
Burnham & Berrow Golf Club

what he saw as the eight weakest holes on the course for completely new
ones. Colt enlisted the help of Dr Alister MacKenzie to redesign both the 9th
and 10th greens, however, only his plans for the 9th green were approved by
the club committee.

More recent changes include new green complexes at the 6th and 16th
holes, carried out by Mackenzie & Ebert in 2013 and 2017.

Throughout its history, Burnham and Berrow has played host to a number
of highly regarded national tournaments including the English Amateur
Championship on six occasions, the Brabazon Trophy (three) and the British
Boys Championship (twice).

PLAYING THE COURSE
If you close your eyes and try to imagine a golf hole that epitomises
everything that is great about traditional, pure, links golf, then it's highly
likely your description would find a perfect match somewhere among the
eighteen that reside on the championship course at Burnham & Berrow.

Tight, undulating fairways set among towering sand dunes – take your
pick. Panoramic sea views off the tee – most definitely. A collection of classic

par-3s – this is a Colt design, would you expect anything less? You'll find all these essential ingredients right here.

As you stand on the 1st tee, you get an immediate sense of the challenge that lies ahead. Like so many links courses, Burnham & Berrow is not a bomber's paradise, rather an examination of positional play from the tee. You'll score better and enjoy your round a whole lot more if you remember that rule.

With the front-9 mainly playing into the prevailing wind, the championship course throws you right in at the deep end with a terrific cluster of opening holes. Your tee-shot at the 1st needs to skirt alongside the large bank on the left of the fairway to leave the best line towards a small, raised, green. Anything right will leave a blind second shot over a sand hill.

Hole 2 is a fabulous par-4 with a narrow, rolling, fairway that winds its way toward the green. Anything pushed left or right off the tee will find trouble. The 3rd hole sets itself as an uphill dogleg left due to the position of the raised tee-box. Any big hitters who fancy a 'boom' here must carry the two bunkers sat at around 230yds, waiting to catch anything that doesn't quite make it. Anyone taking the safer route will be left with a blind approach shot, which needs to thread through two sand hills protecting the green beyond.

Links golf can be brutal at times and the first three holes at Burnham and Berrow are no exception. But just at the point your head may be about to drop, it provides a timely moment of inspiration to lift you back up. If you'd wondered where all the sea views were up to this point, you need wonder no more. At the 4th tee the shoreline reveals itself in quite glorious fashion.

From here you can look out over the Bristol Channel and, on a clear day, catch sight of Cardiff and the South Wales coastline in the distance. To your right, you can see Cheddar Gorge and Glastonbury Tor. Suddenly, the pain from any dropped shots up to now doesn't feel quite so bad.

The 4th hole also provides an element of relief; a par-5 with a generous fairway and no bunkers, offering an immediate opportunity to make a positive mark on your scorecard. Hole 5 is the first of four marvellous par-3s. There are no surprises here; the hole plays exactly as you see it with all the danger at the front of a sloping green. Aim toward the centre or back and you'll be fine.

The newly installed tee-box at the 6th now looks straight down the fairway, rather than from its old location along the left. Sand hills guard the right of the fairway, while thick rough guards the left. Any approach shot needs to avoid the left-hand bunker next to the green.

Before you tee-off at the par-3 9th, be sure to take a look along the coast at the wreck of the SS Nornen, which rests directly behind the back tee and is always visible at low tide. The 9th is a real risk/reward short hole, with a raised green surrounded by six bunkers. There's no other way here other than straight at the flag.

The back-9 has the benefit of the wind coming mainly from behind and starts with a completely blind tee-shot from the 10th. Two marker posts show you the way, depending which tee you go from. Anywhere left of the marker posts will be safe, anything too far right will be lost.

Hole 12 is the famous Church Hole (due to its close proximity to Berrow Parish Church, St Mary's) and it's a tough, uphill, medium length par-4 that plays longer than its yardage suggests. The fairway bends to the right but slopes to the left leaving a tricky tee-shot up the hill. Anything too far right will find rough. It may be worth taking an extra club for your approach toward an elevated two tier green with a steep slope at the front.

The 13th is the final par-5 of the round and a genuine three-shot hole toward a long narrow green with a steep bank off the right-hand side. The 14th is the penultimate par-3. Your tee-shot needs to land along the right to feed off the slope towards the hole.

Berrow Parish Church overlooks the 12th green. *jameslovettphotography.com*

The sun begins to set over the 13th green. *Burnham & Berrow Golf Club*

(17) SIGNATURE HOLE: PAR-3 17TH, 142YDS–202YDS, 'MAJUBA'.
Named after the 1881 battle of Majuba Hill, which took place during the Boer War, and with the Pillar Lighthouse in view directly behind the green. Harry Colt left the best of his wonderful short hole quartet until last.

All of the par-3s at Burnham & Berrow make no apology for goading you with the same question – can you hit the green? If the wind is blowing, take one club more than you think you need as all the trouble is at the front and only a great shot will do.

Before you get to dust yourself down back in the clubhouse, there's the small matter of facing one of the finest closing holes in the UK. A dogleg left with sand dunes all along the right of the fairway. Any draw shot off the tee should run down the fairway leaving a much simpler approach. Anything too long may struggle to hold the green. Only perfection, right at the end, will do.

The 17th green (known as 'Majuba') with the Pillar lighthouse in the background.
Burnham & Berrow Golf Club

Other courses on site

In addition to the Championship course, Burnham and Berrow Golf Club also has the following course available for visitors to play:

● THE CHANNEL COURSE

This 9-hole course (with eighteen different tees available) was designed by Fred Hawtree and opened in 1977. A perfect accompaniment to its elder, 18-hole, sibling.

To book a round for the Channel course use the same options as outlined for the Championship course.

Par: 35 (70: 18 holes)
Length: 2,527yds–2910yds

Green fees:
£20.00 9-holes
£30.00 18-holes

31

SAUNTON GOLF CLUB – EAST COURSE

Braunton,
North Devon,
EX33 1LG.
www.sauntongolf.co.uk
Phone: +44 (0) 1271 812436
Email: info@sauntongolf.co.uk

General course information –
Par: 71 (Blue/White) / 70 (Yellow) / 74 (Red)

S.S.S: 74 (Blue) / 73 (White) / 69 (Yellow) / 76 (Red)

Slope rating: 128 (Blue) / 122 (White) / 116 (Yellow) / 136 (Red)

Length: 5,934yds–6,774yds

Longest hole: Par-5 2nd, 468yds–527yds

Shortest hole: Par-3 5th, 105yds–122yds

Type: Links

Handicap Certificate: Not required (not a course for beginners)

Green fees:
(Low season)
● per round

(Shoulder season)
● per round

(High season)
● per round / day rate

Twilight rate:
● per round (after 2.30pm)

Caddies:
£60.00 per player (+gratuity). Must be booked in advance via email – caddymaster@sauntongolf.co.uk

Equipment hire:
Buggies, trolleys and clubs all available for hire from the pro shop. Recommended to book buggies in advance, if required +44 (0) 1271 812013 / sauntonproshop@foremostgolf.com.

How do I book a round of golf?
Saunton welcomes visitors after 9.30 am, seven days a week.

There are three ways to book a round of golf at Saunton Golf Club:

Online:
www.sauntongolf.co.uk/Visitors/ Book your tee time

Phone:
+44 (0) 1271 812436

Email:
info@sauntongolf.co.uk

Price Guide: ● up to £49 | ● £50 – £99 | ● £100 – £149 | ● £150 – £200 | ● over £200

HISTORY

'Operation Overlord', or D-Day as it is more commonly referred to, commenced on 6 June 1944. It marked the beginning of the allies' march into Nazi Germany, bringing an end to the Second World War.

For the American contingent, the capture of Omaha beach was vital to the success of the overall operation. Planning for D-Day commenced in 1943 and in order for the troops to achieve their objective, they needed to find practice terrain that closely resembled the French coastline where they planned to attack.

Thankfully, an area of land existed in the southwest of England regarded as almost an exact replica of Omaha near the Devon seaside villages of Saunton and Woolacombe.

For six months in the run up to D-Day, these sleepy hamlets came alive with the crackle of gunfire, heavy artillery and military transport, as the US army conducted training exercises over the towering sand dunes of Braunton Burrows.

The 18th green on the East course sits under the shadow of the clubhouse. *Saunton Golf Club*

The local population were more than happy to cater for their visitors, even though it meant their beloved links golf course would become an early casualty with the necessity to prepare for such a large scale military operation bringing a halt to play.

Golf is believed to have been played on the same stretch of land where the East Course now resides as early as 1890. However, Saunton Golf Club was not officially established until 1897. The original course had only 9 holes, extended to 12 holes in 1906, before a further six were added by 1908.

Following a lull during the First World War, the club hired the services of course architect Herbert Fowler, fresh from his earlier success at Walton Heath, to redesign the course layout. To celebrate the opening of the new design an exhibition match took place between Harry Vardon and J.H. Taylor.

Fowler would be called upon again in 1935, this time to design a completely new 18-hole layout, complementing the existing course. Following its completion both courses were given names – East (the original course) and West (the new course).

Both courses suffered immense damage during the Second World War. The land and clubhouse would remain unavailable until 1951. The club soon got to work restoring the East Course to its original state, able to welcome members back to their links paradise by January 1952.

PLAYING THE COURSE

The great links courses are those that instantly remind us that nature was their true architect, man merely found them and shaped them. There's no finer exponent of a course so 'at one' with its natural habitat than the East Course (and West Course, for that matter) at Saunton Golf Club.

When you first arrive at Saunton, take a seat at the front of the clubhouse and allow yourself a few moments to appreciate the splendour of the sprawling landscape stretched across Braunton Burrow's rugged topography.

Harry Vardon, six-time Champion Golfer of the Year and member of the great triumvirate, said that he would happily retire to Saunton and spend the rest of his days playing golf purely for pleasure rather than reward.

Despite the generous fairways, this is a course that requires all the shots in your armoury with many of the greens nestled among sand dunes, or sat high on a plateau above the fairways, demanding accurate approach play. The first 5-holes of the East Course present you with an intense, but immensely enjoyable opening to your round.

The raised tee-box at the 1st gives you a great vantage point of the hole below. Your tee-shot really needs to be either a driver or 3-wood to clear the rough and make it onto the fairway. A cross ditch 60yds from the green may tempt you into laying up, leaving a soft chip onto the green. A five here is not a bad start.

The par-5 2nd is all about your approach shot toward a slightly raised green. Two deep pot bunkers wait, menacingly, at the front to catch anything short, while heavy rough at the back could also wreck a genuine chance to claw back shots dropped at the 1st.

The long par-4 4th (par-5 from the red tees) is the hardest hole on the course. Only a straight drive will do to leave an approach that needs to navigate between a narrow gap in the fairway. Feel free to be bold with your 2nd shot as the landing area beyond this point really opens up toward the green.

The 5th is the signature hole on the front-9, known as 'Tiddler' and Saunton's version of the par-3 'Postage Stamp'. Whatever club you choose, it really must be one that you feel confident will land right in the centre of the green or, at worst, slightly short. Anything off the back of the green will leave one of the most testing shots of the whole round.

The par-4 8th starts with a totally blind tee-shot, but don't be too intimidated as the fairway landing area beyond is pretty wide. Your approach is actually the harder shot, aiming toward a narrow target with the green almost completely surrounded by a ridge of sand dunes.

The back-9 starts with another medium length par-4. The wide fairway leaves you lots of room off the tee but, as with many other holes up to now, your approach shot will define how well you score here. Aiming towards a green atop a plateau (hence the name of the hole) guarded by two bunkers at the front, anything too bold – either short or long – could ruin your scorecard.

As with the 10th (S.I. 18), the par-3 13th (S.I. 14) is a hole that belies its stroke index rating. It's really not that easy. Any tee-shot missing the raised green could find trouble, particularly short (two bunkers guard the front) or long right.

The 18th green on the West course. *Saunton Golf Club*

16 **SIGNATURE HOLE: PAR-4 16TH, 367YDS–435YDS, 'FOWLER'.**
Peter Alliss described the 16th on the East Course as one of his
favourite holes in golf and it's the start of a terrific closing stretch,
bringing you back to the clubhouse. Named after its designer, your
tee-shot is semi-blind and should favour the right side of the fairway
leaving a longer approach towards the green, but as with the 1st hole,
a five on your card here is nothing to be too disappointed with.

The 17th is the final par-3. It's a long one so don't be too concerned about your club choice as there's plenty of room both in front and behind to either be aggressive or safe, leaving a straightforward chip onto the green. Just be sure and hit it straight as bunkers wait both left and right of the green.

The 18th is all about accuracy both off the tee and toward the green sitting in the shadow of the clubhouse. Five bunkers guard the putting surface so nothing less than right at the flag will do for your final approach.

Other courses on site

In addition to the East course, Saunton Golf Club also has the following course available for visitors to play:

● WEST COURSE

Many Saunton members will tell you that if they were asked to make a choice between playing the West or the East course on any given day, it may have to be settled by the toss of a coin.

Abandoned not long after it was first completed in 1935, due to the area's involvement with aiding the war effort, the West Course would have to wait until the mid 1970s before an extensive rebuilding programme orchestrated by Frank Pennink saw it restored and reopened for play.

The West Course has a number of standout holes, in particular the 7th and 8th, both of which still show remnants of when the land was used for something other than golf with evidence of tank tracks running through the fairways.

The tee-box on the par-3 16th is the highest point on either course and provides a wonderful vista back across the whole club. Those who have had the good fortune of playing both courses often feel compelled to make a case for Saunton offering the best 36-hole links experience anywhere in the UK.

To book a round for the West course, use the same options as outlined for the East course.

Par: 71
S.S.S: 71 (White) / 70 (Yellow) / 72 (Red)
Length: 5,314yds–6,596yds

Green fees: Same as East Course.

32

THE ROYAL NORTH DEVON GOLF CLUB, WESTWARD HO!

Golf Links Road,
Westward Ho!,
Bideford, Devon,
EX39 1HD
www.royalnorthdevongolfclub.co.uk
Phone: +44 (0) 1237 473817
Email: info@
royalnorthdevongolfclub.co.uk

General course information –
Par: 72 / 76 (Red)

S.S.S: 75 (Black) / 73 (White) /
72 (Yellow) / 68(M), 76(L) (Red)

Slope rating: 135 (Black) / 134 (White) /
130 (Yellow) / 112 (Red)

Length: 5,709yds–7,000yds

Longest hole: Par-5, 17th (Road)
440yds–554yds

Shortest hole: Par-3 5th (Table)
120yds–163yds

Type: Links

Handicap Certificate: Not required

Green fees:
● per round
● 36 holes (Sun–Fri)

Twilight rate:
● per round (after 4pm)

Caddies:
£40.00 (+ gratuity). Booked
in advance via caddiemaster.
Highly recommended for first time
visitors.

Equipment hire:
Buggies, trolleys and clubs all
available for hire from the pro shop.
Recommended to book buggies in
advance, if required.

How do I book a round of golf?
Royal North Devon welcomes visitors
after 9.30 am, Sunday to Friday and
after 2 pm on Saturdays.

There are three ways to book a
round of golf at Royal North Devon
Golf Club:

Online:
www.royalnorthdevongolfclub.co.uk/
Visitors/Tee Times booking

Phone:
+44 (0) 1237 473817

Email:
info@royalnorthdevongolfclub.co.uk

Price Guide: ● up to £49 | ● £50 – £99 | ● £100 – £149 | ● £150 – £200 | ● over £200

HISTORY

Charles Kingsley was a well-known novelist and clergyman during the Victorian era, serving as chaplain to Queen Victoria and professor of modern history at Cambridge University. In 1854 he moved to the seaside town of Bideford, North Devon, using this new habitat as inspiration for his bestselling novel – *Westward Ho!*.

The book, a historic tale about a young man who sets off on an adventure to do battle with the Spanish Armada, proved so popular that it inspired the development of a new tourist location named in homage to Kingsley's novel – becoming the only town in England with an exclamation mark in its name.

Westward Ho! is now well known for its three-mile stretch of wild, sandy beaches, set along the western side of Bideford Bay, and is very popular with water sports enthusiasts (particularly surfers).

It is also the site of Royal North Devon Golf Club – the birthplace of links golf in England.

The North Devon and West of England Golf Club was officially formed on 4th April 1864, receiving its royal patronage just two years later from HRH Prince of Wales. However, the club's first captain – Rev. Isaac H. Gossett – had

Storm clouds gathering over the wild, natural links at Royal North Devon. *kevinmurraygolfphotography.com*

played golf on the Burrows of Northam with his friends and associates for nearly ten years prior to its formation.

No one knows for sure who designed the original layout, although another founding member, Captain George Molesworth, was alleged to be the architect. Despite the original course having eighteen holes, most rounds were played over twenty-two holes, with many of the fairways crossing over each other.

One of Gossett's playing companions, and brother-in-law, Major General Moncrieff, was also a member of The Royal & Ancient, St Andrews and suggested bringing Old Tom Morris down from Scotland to review the land. Old Tom arrived for a month in 1860 to offer his advice and design a more recognisable course, visiting just once more after the club was formed.

A further redesign took place in 1888, removing all of the remaining criss-crossing fairways and lengthening the course by over 500yds. The layout was modernised once again in 1908 by Herbert Fowler and has largely remained untouched since.

The honours boards hanging around Royal North Devon's clubhouse date back to its foundation and read as a veritable 'who's who' of early golfing pioneers – Horace Hutchinson, Herbert Fowler, Harold Hilton and, perhaps most famous of all, John Henry Taylor, member of the great triumvirate and five times Champion Golfer of the Year.

Born in the nearby village of Northam, it was here that the young, orphaned, Taylor received his tutelage from Horace Hutchinson, first as a caddie boy, then with club in hand, learning the game on the wild links of Westward Ho! before setting out on his quest to become the finest golfer of his generation.

PLAYING THE COURSE

It should come as no surprise that England's most authentic links course provides you with a rich golfing experience unlike any other. At Westward Ho! you don't come just to swing your clubs but to take a nostalgic trip down golf's memory lane.

The most apparent throwback to the good old days is the status of the course as common land (all grazing animals and walkers have right of way) and hence why, standing on the 1st tee, you may feel some extra nerves when you see a herd of sheep happily lunching on the lush green grass across the fairway.

This might be the only course you ever play where local rule No.8, 'Embedded ball and heaped or liquid manure' needs to be enforced. The rule states: 'A ball which lies in or touches heaped or liquid manure may be lifted without penalty, cleaned and dropped...'. It's always reassuring to know such a rule exists should you need it.

For first time visitors, the club strongly recommends either using the services of a caddie or requesting a tee-time with a member of the club. One of the great challenges of this course is knowing where best to aim your ball from the tee and having an experienced voice to guide you is considered a wise move.

The course follows a fairly traditional 'out and back' route with the first two holes taking you from the clubhouse out towards the sea, and the final two bringing you back in.

The par-5 1st is quite a comfortable start with many long hitters able to reach in two. The fairway becomes more undulating toward the green with a ditch very much in play along the left. The par-4 2nd is a long dogleg to the left and the toughest hole on the course. Your tee-shot needs to be straight at the centre of the fairway, which still leaves a tricky approach towards a small green with three bunkers on the right waiting to catch anything pushed in that direction.

Hole 4 is the beginning of a terrific quartet of holes running along the coastline. A medium length par-4 starts with one of golf's great tee shots that must clear two giant fairway bunkers. There's lots of room on this hole offering an early opportunity to be brave with your driver.

The 5th is the first of four par-3s and it's all carry to a large, sloping, green sitting uphill from the tee, guarded on all sides by deep, straight faced bunkers. A par here is a good score.

(6) SIGNATURE HOLE: PAR-4 6TH, 332YDS−412YDS, 'ALP'.
The tee-box at the 6th is the highest point on the course and it's worth taking a moment to appreciate the views out toward Lundy Island and Hartland Point. Your tee shot needs to aim for the right-hand side of a rolling fairway, avoiding bunkers along the left. Aim more left with your approach to safely hit the green, which has quite a severe slope at the front.

The par-4 7th is all about the approach toward a heavily undulating green with four different levels, making your putt extremely difficult to read. Aim your tee shot toward the hut in the distance, splitting the two bunkers sat

The tee-box at the 6th hole (Alp) provides the best view across the rugged links landscape.
Royal North Devon Golf Club

either side of the fairway. Your approach needs to be long, avoiding trouble at the front of the putting surface.

The inward-9 starts with two tricky par-4s. The marker post on the 10th fairway shows you where to go from the tee, avoiding the bunkers along the right-hand side. Four more bunkers protect the front of the green so any approach needs to aim long, but this is a good opportunity to score well if you're on the fairway.

The tee shot at the 11th is regarded as the toughest on the course, particularly when the wind is against you. The fairway looks narrower than it actually is but it simply must be hit, as anything heading into the sea rushes either side will likely be lost.

Hole 14 is a classic par-3 with a 'hog's back' green. Regardless of where the flag position is, aim straight for the centre of the green or lay up short to leave a chip onto the putting surface. A tough closing stretch continues with

View from the tee-box towards the green at the par-3 16th. *Royal North Devon Golf Club*

the long par-4 15th, which doglegs from left to right. Your tee shot has very little to aim at and your approach is usually semi-blind over more sea rushes towards a green sloping front to back.

After the final par-3 at 16, the penultimate hole is the longest on the course. A pretty straight par-5, playing slightly downhill, your approach shot needs to clear a road passing across the fairway in front of the green. Anything pushed or pulled could find a bunker either side.

The closing hole requires a tee shot aiming down the left of the fairway, avoiding the burn separating the 18th and 1st fairways along the right. The burn then runs across the front of the green. Best to play it safe and lay up if you don't think you can clear it with your approach.

33

ST ENODOC GOLF CLUB – CHURCH COURSE

Rock,
Wadebridge,
Cornwall, PL27 6LD
www.st-enodoc.co.uk
Phone: +44 (0) 1208 863216
Email: club@st-enodoc.co.uk

General course information – Men

Par: 69

S.S.S: 73 (Blue) / 72 (White) / 71 (Yellow) / 69 (Red)

Slope rating: 134 (Blue) / 129 (White) / 126 (Yellow) / 118 (Red)

Ladies

Par: 73

S.S.S: 77 (Yellow) / 75 (Red)

Slope rating: 149 (Yellow) / 140 (Red)

Length: 5,644yds–6,557yds

Longest hole: Par-5 16th, 501yds–560yds

Shortest hole: Par-3 8th, 130yds–165yds

Type: Links

Handicap Certificate: Required (maximum 24 for men and 28 for ladies)

Green fees:
(Low season)
● per round

(High season)
● per round (Weekday)
● per round (Weekend)
● one round on each course

Caddies:
£55.00 (+ gratuity). Must be booked in advance via Secretary's office.

Equipment hire:
Buggies are available if required on medical grounds and should be booked in advance. Clubs and trolleys can be hired from the pro shop.

How do I book a round of golf?
St Enodoc welcomes visitors at all times during the week to play the Church Course.

There are three ways to book a round of golf at St Enodoc Golf Club:

Online:
www.st-enodoc.co.uk / Tee Time Booking

Phone:
+44 (0) 1208 863216

Email:
enquiries@st-enodoc.co.uk

Price Guide: ● up to £49 | ● £50 – £99 | ● £100 – £149 | ● £150 – £200 | ● over £200

HISTORY

'Sinking Neddy' is not a nickname you'd typically associate with a church; nonetheless, local residents in the Cornish parish of St Minver deemed it quite appropriate for their place of worship.

Believed to date back as far as the twelfth century, St Enodoc Church lay partially buried by shifting sand dunes for over 300 years before a major excavation in 1864. Prior to its restoration, in order for it to remain consecrated, the vicar was lowered through a skylight in the roof so he could carry out a blessing.

For the last 130 years, the chapel, with its distinctive crooked spire, has become an iconic image associated with the golf course – known since 1987 as the Church Course – that now surrounds it.

Stunning aerial view of the 9th and 16th fairways with the 15th green, bottom-left. *St Enodoc Golf Club*

Formed in 1890, St Enodoc Golf Club began its life with a small membership of just twenty who played their golf over twenty-seven holes – 18 out and 9 in. In 1907, the club invited revered architect James Braid to design a new 18-hole layout (Braid submitted two designs, one of which became the Church Course).

After alterations in the 1920s by Herbert Fowler and Tom Simpson, Braid returned in the mid-1930s to reconstruct the 17th and 18th holes and make room for the existing clubhouse, opened in 1937. The Church Course has remained relatively untouched since these alterations.

In 2002, five-time Open champion Tom Watson visited his old friend, Thomas 'Tuck' Clagett, general manager of St Enodoc at the time for a round of golf. So entranced by the course, Tom gave the club his wedge as a gift. Every year since, members have a chance to get their hands on Tom's old club (which hangs proudly in the clubhouse) when they play in the annual 'Tom Watson Wedge' stableford competition.

PLAYING THE COURSE

Two much-admired 'men of letters' were so inspired by their encounter with the Church Course they felt compelled to pay their own personal homage.

Poet laureate Sir John Betjeman owned a house near the 12th hole, becoming an honorary member of St Enodoc in 1977. Betjeman held a lifelong love of Cornwall and his home golf course; hence, he did what all great poets would do, he wrote a poem about it.

How straight it flew, how long it flew,
It clear'd the rutty track
And soaring, disappeared from view
Beyond the bunker's back –
A glorious, sailing, bounding drive
That made me glad I was alive...
... Lark song and sea sounds in the air
And splendour, splendour everywhere.

'Seaside Golf' (abridged version), Sir John Betjeman.

In his book *A Course Called Scotland*, Tom Coyne takes a detour around the southwest of England before heading north and describes his visit to St Enodoc as 'a golf dream from which one would wake in tears for its having come to an end, a course stretched along a coastline that had literally been blessed by golf.'

If such remarkable articulation requires any further clarity let it simply be said: a round of golf at St Enodoc lives long in the memory.

Set on a rugged hillside among towering sand dunes, across the Camel estuary from the picturesque seaside town of Padstow, the Church Course offers some of the most innovative, natural, routeing you'll find anywhere in the British Isles.

Don't be fooled by what may appear a modest overall yardage – this is a challenging walk, compensated by the most majestic views over Daymer Bay. Before you catch your first glimpse of the sea, there's the small matter of a rare par-5 opening hole.

As you stand on the 1st tee, the fairway resembles what can only be described as a mini mountain range, making it tricky to see any clear landing area. Anything in the middle or slightly left will be fine. Your second shot is blind as the fairway slopes down toward the green. Aim left of the marker post to leave the best approach.

The 3rd hole is a delightful downhill dogleg left par-4. Your tee-shot needs to stay right of the fairway for the best line towards a green sitting behind an old Cornish wall. Anything pushed too far right could end up out of bounds.

Hole 4 is another fabulous par-4 dogleg left, this time uphill. Out of bounds again lurks all along the right. The green sits next to farmland

Looking towards the 6th hole and the enormous 'Himalaya' dune complex with the green in the far distance. *kevinmurraygolfphotography.com*

regularly used for cow grazing so don't be nervous if you play this hole in front of some unexpected spectators.

Of the four par-3s on the course, the heavenly backdrops at both the 5th and 15th holes make it borderline unfair to then demand the solid tee shot required in order to land on the green. For a good score at the 5th, try and aim for the right side of the putting surface.

The 6th is the front-9's signature hole, played around the famous Himalaya complex. Aim left of the fairway if you want to go around the huge sand dune. If you're feeling brave you're more than welcome to aim right, leaving a completely blind approach shot that needs to clear the ridge with plenty to spare.

The smart move is to take an extra club for your approach as anything short leaves a tricky pitch towards quite a small, raised green.

(10) SIGNATURE HOLE: PAR-4 (PAR-5 FROM THE RED TEES) 10TH, 449YDS–457YDS.

As you commence the back-9, St Enodoc Church finally comes into view. This part of the course morphs into a hybrid links/moorland test with holes 10 through to 15 located in the shadow of Brea Hill.

Not only is the 10th hole the hardest on the Church Course, it's often regarded by many who play it to be the toughest par-4 they've played anywhere. Rather ironically, as it sits in sight of a church, this is a hole that does not often allow you to repent your golfing sins.

Your tee-shot must be nothing less than straight and long to reach the narrow fairway flanked by a stream on the left and towering sand dunes all along the right. For long hitters any approach shot needs to aim back over the stream toward the green.

For high handicappers, playing this hole as a par-5 is the smart move, aiming your second shot toward the church spire to leave a pitch on to the putting surface.

Any par score here (either 4's or 5's) should be followed by a detour into the church for a brief prayer as attaining them on this hole often requires divine intervention.

The par-4 13th provided the inspiration for Sir John Betjeman's poem, 'Seaside Golf', after he achieved a rare birdie score. While not a long hole, it has quite a steep incline with out of bounds all along the left adding considerable difficulty, requiring total concentration and accurate club selection.

View that greets you at the 10th fairway looking towards St Enodoc Church. *St Enodoc Golf Club*

After a terrific par-3 at the 15th, with a downhill tee shot toward a green well protected by pot bunkers left and right, the course moves back alongside the estuary for the final three holes.

The 16th is the longest hole on the course demanding a solid tee-shot toward the top of a plateau. Your second shot is blind and needs to keep right to avoid fairway bunkers along the left. The green is also well protected with bunkers at the front and thick rough off the back.

Hole 17 is the final par-3 and it's a long one, all uphill and all carry. Nothing less than right at the centre of the green will do if you're to achieve a good score. A severe bunker sits menacingly front-right ready to catch anything pushed in that direction. Take an extra club and aim more toward the back to be safe.

A tough par-4 brings a close to the round. Your tee-shot needs to split the two sand dunes sitting either side of a narrow section of the fairway. Your final approach needs to avoid bunkers protecting either side of the green if you're to finish with a flourish.

Stunning sunset over the 16th hole at St Enodoc. *jameslovettphotography.com*

Other courses on site

In addition to the Church Course, St Enodoc Golf Club also has the following course available for visitors to play:

● HOLYWELL COURSE

Designed by James Braid in 1928, originally as a 9-hole course. Abandoned during the Second World War, the Holywell reopened in 1967 and was extended to 18 holes in 1982.

Ideal for beginners and younger golfers looking to test their game on a less demanding layout than the Church Course. The par-3 15th on the Holywell is regarded by many as the toughest short hole on the complex.

To book a round for the Holywell Course, use the same options as outlined for the Church Course.

Par: 63
S.S.S: 61
Length: 4,082yds

Green fees:
● per round / day rate

18-hole courses nearby

● TREVOSE GOLF & COUNTRY CLUB – CHAMPIONSHIP COURSE

Opened in 1925 and originally designed by Harry Colt. The course is laid out as two 9-hole loops, the outward-9 hugs the coastline and provides spectacular views of the Atlantic and the inward-9 brings you back inland. A very challenging round of golf, at just over 7,000yds, particularly when the wind is blowing.

In addition to the championship course, the complex also has two smaller 9-hole courses available for visitors to play.

Website: www.trevose-gc.co.uk
Email: info@trevose-gc.co.uk
Phone: + 44 (0) 1841 520208

Par: 72 / 73 (Red)
Length: 5,819yds–7,079yds
Type: Links

Fees:
● per round

● PERRANPORTH GOLF CLUB

A links course designed by James Braid that has been left largely untouched since opening for play in 1927 – what more incentive could you need to want to play here? It also provides pretty dramatic views across the Atlantic coastline.

Website: www.perranporthgolfclub. co.uk
Phone: +44 (0) 1872 572454

Par: 72 (White/Red) / 70 (Yellow)
Length: 5,302yds–6,296yds
Type: Links

Fees:
● per round

Aerial view of the 4th hole at Trevose Golf & Country Club. *jameslovettphotography.com*

Aerial view of the links course at Perranporth Golf Club. *Perranporth Golf Club*